OBLIGED BY MEMORY

Religion, Theology, and the Holocaust
Steven T. Katz, *Series Editor*

Other titles in Religion, Theology, and the Holocaust

Absence/Presence: Essays and Reflections on the Artistic Memory of the Holocaust
   Stephen Feinstein
Act and Idea in the Nazi Genocide. Berel Lang
Christian Responses to the Holocaust: Moral and Ethical Issues. Donald J. Dietrich
The End of Days: A Memoir of the Holocaust. Helen Sendyk
Himmler's Jewish Taylor: The Story of Holocaust Survivor Jacob Frank
   Jacob Frank, with Mark Lewis
Life in the Ghettos During the Holocaust. Eric J. Sterling, ed.
The Man Who Stopped the Trains to Auschwitz: George Mantello, El Salvador, and Switzerland's Finest Hour. David Kranzler
The Meeting: An Auschwitz Survivor Confronts an SS Physician
   Bernhard Frankfurter, ed.; Susan E. Cernyak-Spatz, trans.
My War: Memoir of a Young Jewish Poet. Edward Stankiewicz
New Dawn: The Triumph of Life after the Holocaust. Helen Sendyk
Nightmares: Memoirs of the Years of Horror under Nazi Rule in Europe, 1939–1945
   Konrad Charmatz; Miriam Dashkin Beckerman, trans.
Second Generation Voices: Reflections by Children of Holocaust Survivors and Perpetrators
   Alan L. Berger and Naomi Berger, eds.
Survival: The Story of a Sixteen-year-old Jewish Boy. Israel J. Rosengarten
Three Homelands: Memories of a Jewish Life in Poland, Israel, and America
   Norman Salsitz, with Stanley Kaish
War in the Shadow of Auschwitz: Memoirs of a Polish Resistance Fighter and Survivor of the Death Camps. John Wiernicki
Who Will Say Kaddish? A Search for Jewish Identity in Contemporary Poland
   Larry N. Mayer, Text; Gary Gelb, Photographs
Will to Freedom: A Perilous Journey Through Facism and Communism
   Egon Balas
The Warriors: My Life as a Jewish Soviet Partisan. Harold Zissman

Obliged by Memory

LITERATURE, RELIGION, ETHICS

•

*A collection of essays honoring
Elie Wiesel's seventieth birthday*

•

Edited by
Steven T. Katz *and* Alan Rosen

SYRACUSE UNIVERSITY PRESS

Copyright © 2006 by Syracuse University Press
Syracuse, New York 13244-5160

All Rights Reserved

First Edition 2006

06 07 08 09 10 11   6 5 4 3 2 1

The paper used in this publication meets the minimum
requirements of American National Standard for Information
Sciences—Permanence of Paper for Printed Library Materials,
ANSI Z39.48–1984.∞ ™

Library of Congress Cataloging-in-Publication Data

Obliged by memory : literature, religion, ethics / edited by Steven T. Katz
and Alan Rosen.—1st ed.
    p. cm.—(Religion, theology, and the Holocaust)
  Includes bibliographical references and index.
  ISBN 0-8156-3064-6 (alk. paper)
  1. Holocaust, Jewish 1939–1945—Influence—Congresses. 2. Holocaust, Jewish (1939–1945)—Moral and ethical aspects—Congresses. 3. Holocaust, Jewish (1939–1945), in literature—Congresses. I. Katz, Steven T., 1944–
II. Rosen, Alan. III. Series.
D804.18.025   2005
940.53'18019—dc22
                2005026102

Manufactured in the United States of America

Contents

Preface
    ALAN ROSEN   vii

Contributors   ix

Introduction
    ALAN ROSEN   xiii

Writing, Memory, and the Word

1. The Rights of History and the Rights of Imagination
    CYNTHIA OZICK   3

Memory and Memoirs

2. Do Facts Matter in Holocaust Memoirs? Wilkomirski/Wiesel
    SUSAN RUBIN SULEIMAN   21

3. The Advantages of Delay: A Psychological Perspective on Memoirs of Trauma
    SHLOMO BREZNITZ   43

Memory, History, Ethics

4. Memory, History, and Ethics
    JOHN SILBER   55

Memory and the Persecutor

5. *Reflections on the Papon Trial*
   JEFFREY MEHLMAN   69

6. *The Grey Zone of Scientific Invention: Primo Levi and the Omissions of Memory*
   NANCY HARROWITZ   83

Memory and the Victim

7. *Elie Wiesel and the Morality of Fiction*
   GEOFFREY HARTMAN   107

8. *Transfusing Memory: Second Generation Postmemory in Elie Wiesel's* The Forgotten
   ALAN L. BERGER   117

Memory and God

9. *Augustine on God and Memory*
   PAULA FREDRIKSEN   131

10. *God's Memory*
    NEHEMIA POLEN   139

On Memory and the Holocaust

Afterword
   ELIE WIESEL   157

Works Cited   165

Index   175

Preface

THE ESSAYS INCLUDED HEREIN were initially presented at a symposium convened in honor of Elie Wiesel's seventieth birthday. Over three days, lecturers addressed the issue of memory from multiple vantage points. At the close of each day, Wiesel responded. The present volume keeps the focus on memory, and particularly memory in relation to the Holocaust. It also tries to preserve something of the flavor of the exchange that took place during those days.

The title of the symposium, "The Claims of Memory," was meant to convey the omnipresence of memory in Elie Wiesel's writing. Memory dominates Wiesel's writing, both in terms of form—the crucial role of the memoir in his oeuvre—and in terms of theme—his preoccupation with memory in his fiction and essays. The present volume, *Obliged by Memory*, continues to elaborate the claims that his work on (and, rightly said, on behalf of) memory make upon his readers. In some cases, authors address Wiesel's contribution directly; in other cases, authors' concerns implicitly reflect and refract Wiesel's own.

It is difficult to imagine an intellectual setting today in which the issue of memory does not play a pivotal role. It would be a different story had Elie Wiesel not placed memory, and particularly memory of the Holocaust, at the center of his and our agenda. This volume pays tribute to his efforts while indicating some of the paths and byways his legacy has taken.

Contributors

Alan L. Berger occupies the Raddock Eminent Scholar Chair for Holocaust Studies and is professor of Judaic studies at Florida Atlantic University. Among his books are *Crisis and Covenant: The Holocaust in American Jewish Fiction* and *Children of Job: American Second-Generation Witnesses to the Holocaust*, and, as editor, *Judaism in the Modern World*.

Shlomo Breznitz is professor of psychology at the University of Haifa and at New School University. He is the author of *Memory Fields* and *Handbook of Stress*.

Paula Fredriksen is the Aurelio Professor of Scripture at Boston University. A specialist in the history of ancient Christianity, she has written books on Augustine, on Jesus, and on Christian origins. Her most recent book is *Augustine and the Jews*.

Nancy Harrowitz is associate professor of Italian at Boston University. She has written *The Logic of Cultural Difference: Cesare Lombroso and Matilde Serao*, edited *Tainted Greatness: Antisemitism and Cultural Heroes*, and coedited *Jews and Gender: Responses to Otto Weininger*. She has also written several articles on Primo Levi and is currently working on a book on science and Levi.

x / Contributors

Geoffrey Hartman is Sterling Professor of English and Comparative Literature, emeritus, and senior research scholar at Yale University. At Yale he cofounded the Fortunoff Archive for Holocaust Testimony. He is the author most recently of *Scars of the Spirit: The Struggle Against Inauthenticity* and *The Geoffrey Hartman Reader*. He was recently elected as a Corresponding Fellow of the British Academy.

Steven T. Katz is director of the Elie Wiesel Center for Judaic Studies at Boston University. His many publications include *Post-Holocaust Dialogues*, which won the National Jewish Book Award in 1984; and a multivolume study, *The Holocaust in Historical Context*, of which volume 1 appeared in 1994. He is the editor of the journal *Modern Judaism*.

Jeffrey Mehlman is university professor and professor of French literature at Boston University. He is the author, most recently, of *Walter Benjamin for Children: An Essay on His Radio Years; Genealogies of the Text: Literature Politics and Psychoanalysis in Modern France*, and *Émigré New York: French Intellectuals in Wartime Manhattan*.

Cynthia Ozick is the author of novels, stories, and essays, including most recently *Heir to the Glimmering World* and *Quarrel and Quandary: Essays*.

Nehemia Polen is professor of Jewish thought and director of the Hasidic Text Institute at Boston's Hebrew College. He is the author of *The Holy Fire: The Teachings of Rabbi Kalonymus Kalman Shapira, the Rebbe of the Warsaw Ghetto; The Rebbe's Daughter;* and, with Lawrence Kushner, *Filling Words with Light: Hasidic and Mystical Reflections on Jewish Prayer*.

Alan Rosen was a 2004–05 Meltzer Research Fellow, Center for Advanced Judaic Studies, University of Pennsylvania, and the 2004–05

Sosland Fellow, Center for Advanced Holocaust Studies, United States Holocaust Memorial Museum. He is the author most recently of *Sounds of Defiance: The Holocaust, Multilingualism, and the Problem of English*.

John Silber is president emeritus, university professor, and professor of philosophy and law at Boston University. He is the author of *Straight Shooting; Democracy: Its Counterfeits and Its Promise*, and "The Ethical Significance of Kant's Religion" in addition to numerous articles on Kant, on education, and on social, political, and foreign policy issues.

Susan Rubin Suleiman is the C. Douglas Dillon Professor of the Civilization of France and professor of comparative literature at Harvard. Her books include *Risking Who One Is: Encounters with Contemporary Art and Literature, Budapest Diary: In Search of the Motherbook, Crises of Memory and the Second World War*, and the edited volume *Exile and Creativity: Signposts, Travelers, Outsiders, Backward Glances*. She is coeditor of *Contemporary Jewish Writing in Hungary: An Anthology*.

Elie Wiesel is the Andrew W. Mellon Professor of Humanities at Boston University. He is the author of over forty books, including most recently *Wise Men and Their Tales: Portraits of Biblical, Talmudic and Hasidic Masters* and *The Time of the Uprooted*.

Introduction

WITH TWO IMPORTANT EXCEPTIONS, the essays included in this volume address what might be called the strategies of memory in relation to the Holocaust, taking up issues of media and genre, aesthetics and ethics, national memory and disciplinary memory. This is not the first book to examine links between memory and the Holocaust. Indeed, as citations and references show, it appreciatively draws on forerunners. But the emphasis is different. Whereas earlier volumes place the Holocaust first and then turn to the coloring that memory adds, *Obliged by Memory* begins with memory and proceeds to the Holocaust.

Several essays evaluate the complex act of representing the Holocaust in different media—writing, image, and film—and in different genres—memoir, history, and fiction. Surprisingly, author Cynthia Ozick argues for the preeminence of the camera image for accurate representation of Holocaust memory. Behind her assessment lie the manipulations and distortions to which writing has subjected the Holocaust: "You could not quarrel with the pictures. You could not change what they insistently and irremediably saw. But as the words rushed in in torrents, as they proliferated, becoming more and more various and removed, some broke through the gates of memory into the freer fields of parable, myth, analogy, symbol, story."

The complicated case of Binjamin Wilkomirski's book *Fragments* serves as one of Ozick's examples of where fiction fails to realize that it isn't memory. Wilkomirski put forward his book as a memoir of his own experience as a young child in a concentration camp. Critics have demonstrated that Wilkomirski is likely not who he claims to be and that he probably never endured the experiences his book recounts. Ozick believes that the Wilkomirski case shows how easily written narrative can lose sight of its boundaries, mistaking fabrication for fact.

The murky status of Wilkomirski's book also is at the forefront of Susan Rubin Suleiman's inquiry. But Suleiman prefers to try to fathom what the ambiguous position of *Fragments* can suggest regarding the indefinite relation of fact and fiction: "As an extreme case," writes Suleiman, *Fragments* "poses certain questions starkly: where does literature end (or begin) and psychopathology begin (or end)? Where should the line be drawn—should the line be drawn?—between personal memory and 'borrowed' memory? To whom does the memory of the Holocaust belong?"

Many would argue that, in our day, memory still belongs preeminently to the survivors. In turning to the very different situation of Elie Wiesel, Suleiman examines how fact and fiction play a role in survivor Wiesel's rewriting of his Holocaust experience in early and later memoirs. Wiesel corrected in his later memoir a detail about deportation that appeared in the earlier one. Suleiman shows how Wiesel's revision of his earlier account gives a fuller portrait of what it means to write a memoir of the Holocaust. Importantly, Wiesel indicated that other survivors challenged his first version; it was their command of a communal memory that moved him to redress the inaccuracy. Hence, Wiesel's rewriting might be seen as moving toward a kind of *yizkhor buch*, a communal enterprise of recollection wherein those who were on the scene of the events can together forge a collective memory.

. . .

If memory is potent in claiming a hold on the past, these essays also suggest that memory is profoundly subject to distortions, vulnerable to the infiltration of images that often present themselves as memory even though they are not. Historians of the Holocaust have generally been suspicious of memory, preferring the quotidian nature of document over the untethered nature of memory. This suspicion has been voiced particularly in relation to memoirs, written or oral, that survivors have recorded years after the events. The presumption is that the passage of time blurs what happened and makes it difficult to discriminate between what one experienced and what one has read or heard.

But what if, suggests Shlomo Breznitz, the passage of time actually works to make memory not less but more accurate, to make the memoir written years after the events more rather than less valuable? Himself the author of a memoir written some fifty years after the events it recounts, Breznitz reflects on the "advantages of delay," as he terms them. In Breznitz's compelling assessment, time acts as a filtering agent, freeing memory of youthful excesses that could distend it. Although the author writes out of his own experience, his reversal of the common (and, likely, commonsense) evaluation of time and memory pleads implicitly for a reassessment of the many instances of belated testimony. It may be that being distant in time is made up for in the sobriety with which mature memory sifts the past.

Distortion may nonetheless falsify memory by other means. Indeed, memory can be falsified not only by what is imported in but also by what is left out. The risk is greatest, John Silber suggests, when the last witness has disappeared from the scene. At that point, history can run amok, forsaking its vocation as "surrogate memory," in Silber's evocative phrase. But transgressions of this kind occur as well while the witnesses live. The absence of a reference to Jews as victims at the commemorative site of Babi Yar, for instance, made it not only a place at which evil had been perpetrated but also a locale notorious for its falsification of history. The second evil was not as bloody as the first but was perhaps equally ethically scandalous.

Yet in different cases, such significant omissions can be subtle—almost, one is tempted to say, innocent—as well. Nancy Harrowitz argues that one can find, and learn from, such omissions in the work of Primo Levi. A scientist as well as a storyteller, Levi, according to Harrowitz, left out of his castigation of modern science its ignoble contribution to the operation of the concentration camps. More than anything, Levi's omissions suggest the strain under which he attempted to harmonize his dual vocations. Mostly able to uniquely blend the realms of science and art, Levi was at a deeper level trying to come to terms with the terrible legacy that science bequeathed.

The efforts to homogenize national memory intensify the strain visible on the individual level. Each nation filters and accommodates in its own way to produce a version of collective national identity. France, as a nation that both capitulated and resisted during World War II, faces a more difficult task than most in confronting the Holocaust. By chronicling the intricacies of the trial of Maurice Papon, Jeffrey Mehlman exposes the fissures in France's memory of its Holocaust past, an evolving memory in which France at first highlighted resistance and only later admitted its collaboration with the perpetrators. En route, Mehlman shows how political trials dramatize and forge memory.

A too-intent focus on memory's fallibility, however, is liable to make us miss the essential life-giving power that it possesses. The annihilating force of the Holocaust highlights how necessary this power is—how the resurrecting energy that memory unleashes is perhaps the most fitting response to evil. Hence, in two pivotal essays, Geoffrey Hartman and Alan L. Berger trace the potency of memory in the writing of Elie Wiesel, delineating the way this potency underlies the very notion of character in Wiesel's fiction. As Hartman comments, "Memory should become, Wiesel has said, an 'irresistible power,' one that gives the dead their due, that tells their story—rather, brings them back to tell their story, even if it was buried with them in an unknown place." Memory thus implies more than recalling what one knows oneself. It means inventing a memory for those who did not survive. In his fiction, then, Wiesel perceives what one might call latent memories—memories that might (or would) have been—and fills in their outlines. This is what Hartman justly calls Wiesel's "morality of fiction." Resurrecting the dead and inventing memories on their behalf thus set a standard for a moral response. Berger's focus on memory "transfusion" in Wiesel's haunting novel *The Forgotten* complements Hartman's, and details the urgent effort to transfer memory from one generation to the next. As Wiesel's insistence on the force of forgetting implies, the act of bestowing memory on a generation that was not there takes its own special powers of imagination and invention.

The concluding two essays, by Paula Fredriksen and Nehemia Polen, ask, "Does God have a memory?" and explore what kind of memory this is, or would be. Shifting the focus from human to divine memory works a kind of estrangement, a questioning of what memory is by asking, "To whom does it belong?" As a taken for granted part of the "human" apparatus of conjuring the past that is taken for granted, memory may be, strikingly, something alien to God, something that human beings—less than and different from the Creator—have a patent on. If so, what particular aspect of the human predicament is memory responsible for? If not—if God indeed has a memory, if memory is not a faculty owned by humanity alone but rather is something shared between creature and Creator (as both essays argue)—what does that joint ownership, as it were, suggest about the nature and role of memory?

Fredriksen and Polen pursue the question by way of two texts from antiquity, the biblical book of Nehemiah and the autobiographical *Confessions of Augustine*. Ancient though these texts may be, their protagonists take on a modern cast in both essays. Indeed, the two featured texts set forth the twin poles of memory on which the later texts depend: first, the anxious inquiry into the place of the nation in the advent of a new era; and second, the inward scrutiny of personal memory to gauge where one stands. These essays thus delineate foundational elements, ancient models of collective and individual memory that, at moments of profound crisis, continue to give us our bearings. They both illuminate what we believe memory to be, and help us to understand what would be lost if memory is lost. Asking questions about God's memory thus becomes another way of ferreting out the nature of the human.

These ten essays, then, together with Elie Wiesel's afterword, explore the complicated relationships between memory and witness, witness and history. In both the questions they raise and the connections they make, the authors articulate the centrality of memory, not only in terms of the Holocaust, but as a process at the ethical center of being human.

♦ Writing, Memory, and the Word ♦

1

The Rights of History and the Rights of Imagination

CYNTHIA OZICK

IT WAS NOT THROUGH WORDS that the world first took in the nature and degree of the atrocities wreaked upon Jews by Germans a half-century ago. You could not read of the last and worst of these atrocities in the newspaper of record, which suppressed reports of such events even as they were occurring, but certain early depredations you could glimpse, fleetingly, in the newsreels: the crowns of fire and smoke bursting through the roofs of burning synagogues on the night of November 9, 1938, the pyres of burning books in the city squares, the genial faces of young men as they hurled intellect into the flames. Sitting peacefully in an American movie house, you could see all these things with your own eyes, and—through film's illusion of simultaneity—you can see these same scenes today.

The burning synagogues and the burning books are what are currently termed icons—incarnations of a time when, nearly all over Europe, Jews were becoming defenseless human prey. Other images are equally indelible: the photo of the terror-stricken little boy with his cap askew and his hands in the air (impossible not to absorb those desperate eyes, those small elbows, that civilized cap, without belief in the true existence of absolute evil); and, at war's end, the hellish frames of a British bulldozer shoveling a hill of skeletal human corpses into a ditch. In the film the bulldozer blunders forward and shovels, backs up, repositions itself, and shovels again. The camera will admit us to these horrors as often as we dare to revisit them. And we must suppose that some of these images, through repetition, have become so recognizable, so clichéd, that the most liberal hearts can be hardened against them. I recall a private letter from a celebrated novelist: "These old events," he wrote, "can rake you over only so much, and then you long for a bit of satire on it all." Satire?

There is another image less well known than the fires and the boy and the bulldozer; it is more overtly brutish by virtue of its being less overtly brutish. And if satire means a parody of normality, then perhaps this scene is travesty enough to gratify the most jaded observer. A city street, modern and clean, lined with leafy bushes and arching trees, on a fine bright autumn day. The road has been cleared of cars to make room for a parade. The marchers are all men, fathers and breadwinners, middle-class burghers wearing the long overcoats and gray fedoras of the thirties; they appear gentlemanly but somber. Along the parade route, behind mild barriers, a cheerful citizenry watches, looking as respectable as the marchers themselves, all nicely dressed, men and women and children, but mostly women and children—these are, let us note, business hours, when fathers and breadwinners are ordinarily in their offices. The weather is lovely, the crowds are pleasant, the women are laughing, the marchers are grave; here and there you will notice a child darting past the barriers, on a dare. The marchers are Jews being taken away in a scheme preparatory for their destruction; they are being escorted by soldiers with guns. Perhaps the watchers do not yet know the destiny of the marchers; but what a diversion it is, what a holiday, to see these dignified gentlemen humiliated, like clowns on show, by the power of the gun!

We may tremble before these images, but we are morally obliged to the German lens that inscribed them. The German lens recorded truthfully; its images are stable and trustworthy: the camera and the act are irrevocably twinned. Though photography can be kin to forgery (consider only the egregious slantedness of so many contemporary "documentaries"), at that time the camera did not lie. It yielded—and preserved—an account of ineffaceable clarity and immutable integrity. And later, when the words disclosing those acts of oppression first began to arrive, we knew them to be as stable and as trustworthy as the camera's images. The scrupulous voice of Elie Wiesel; the scrupulous voice of Primo Levi; the stumbling voices of witnesses who have no fame and have no voice, yet whose eloquence rises up through the scars and stammerings of remembered suffering. The voices of Christian conscience and remorse. All these words were consequential in a way the pictures were not. The pictures belonged to their instant; though they could serve memory, they were not the same as memory. You could not quarrel with the pictures. You could not change what they insistently and irremediably saw. But as the words rushed in in torrents, as they proliferated, becoming more and more various and removed, some broke through the gates of memory into the freer fields of parable, myth, analogy, symbol, story. And where memory was fastidious in honoring history, story turned to the other muses. Where memory was strict, fiction could be lenient, and sometimes lax. Where memory struggled for stringency of historical precision, fiction drifted toward history as a thing to be used, as imagination's stimulus and provocation.

And just here is the crux: the aims of imagination are not the aims of history. Scholars are nowadays calling historiography into radical question; history is seen as the historian's clay; omniscience is suspect, objectivity is suspect, the old-fashioned claims of historical truthfulness are suspect; the causes of the Peloponnesian War are sometimes what I say they are, and sometimes what you say they are. But even under the broken umbrella of contemporary relativism, history has not yet been metamorphosed into fable. Scholars may not agree on what happened, but they do consent to an actual happening. Your Napoleon may not be my Napoleon, but the fact of Napoleon is incontrovertible. To whatever degree, history is that which is owed to reality.

Imagination—fiction—is freer than that; is freed altogether. Fiction has license to do anything it pleases. Fiction is liberty at its purest. It can, if it likes—in the manner of *A Connecticut Yankee in King Arthur's Court*, or Mel Brooks in the French Revolution—place Napoleon in command of the armies of Sparta. It can alter history; it can invent a history that never was, as long as it maintains a hint of verisimilitude. A fictional character represents only itself. You may be acquainted with someone "like" Emma Bovary or "like" Anna Karenina, but if you want the true and only Bovary, you must look to Flaubert, and if you want the true and only Karenina, you must look to Tolstoy. Bovary is not a stand-in for French women; she is Flaubert's invention. Karenina is not a stand-in for Russian women; she is Tolstoy's invention. Imagination owes nothing to what we call reality; it owes nothing to history. The phrase "historical novel" is mainly an oxymoron. History is rooted in document and archive. History is what we make out of memory. Fiction flees libraries and loves lies.

The rights of fiction are not the rights of history.

On what basis, then, can I disdain a story that subverts document and archive? On what basis can I protest a novel that falsifies memory? If fiction annihilates fact, that is the imagination's prerogative. If fiction evades plausibility, that too is the imagination's prerogative. And if memory is passionate in its adherence to history, why should that impinge on the rights of fiction? Why should the make-believe people in novels be obliged to concur with history, or to confirm it? Characters in fiction are not illustrations or representations. They are freely imagined fabrications; they have nothing to do with the living or the dead; they go their own way. And there the matter ends; or should. Nothing is at issue. But there are, admittedly, certain difficulties. Embedded in the idea of fiction is impersonation: every novelist enters the personae of his or her characters; fiction writing is make-believe, acting a part, assuming an identity not one's own. Novelists are, after all, professional impostors; they become the people they invent. When the imposture remains within the confines of a book, we call it art. But when impersonation escapes the bounds of fiction and invades life, we call it hoax—or, sometimes, fraud. Three recent exemplars have captured public attention; all have provoked argument and controversy.

In 1995, Alan Dershowitz, famed equally for his contribution to the legal defense of O. J. Simpson and for his authorship of books of Jewish self-consciousness, published a review of *The Hand That Signed the Papers*, an Australian novel on a Ukrainian theme. Dershowitz took issue with both plot and substance, and accused the twenty-four-year-old writer, Helen Demidenko, of "the most primitive manifestations of classic Ukrainian anti-Semitism: all Jews are Communists, cheats, smelly animals and otherwise subhuman." According to Dershowitz's summary of the novel, when the Soviet commissars—all Jews—arrive in Ukraine in the 1930s, they burn down a house with a family inside; understandably, the surviving child becomes the so-called Ivan the Terrible of Treblinka. A Jewish woman from Leningrad, Dershowitz's account continues, "refuses to treat a sick Ukrainian baby, declaring 'I am a physician, not a veterinarian.' " Demidenko's "subtle goal," he concludes, is "to explain the Ukrainian participation in the Holocaust so that the murders go unpunished," and her "greatest anger is directed against the Jewish survivors who sought to bring their Ukrainian tormentors to justice."

Soon after the appearance of Dershowitz's review, the Australian Federation of Ukrainian Organizations threatened to bring a legal action against him under Australia's racial vilification law. Dershowitz responded by welcoming a lawsuit as "an excellent forum for reminding the world of the complicity of so many Ukrainians in the Nazi Holocaust." That the dispute concerned a work of fiction appeared to vanish in the legal and political tumult. Meanwhile, however, the novel rose to fourth on Australia's best-seller list and received the country's most prestigious literary prize, the Miles Franklin Award. The judges praised Demidenko for illuminating "a hitherto unspeakable portion of the Australian migrant experience." Demidenko herself insisted that her story was based on her own family's travail.

As it turned out, all parties were duped: the protesting reviewer, the infuriated Ukrainians, the publisher, the prize-givers. Helen Demidenko was in reality Helen Darville, a daughter of British immigrants pretending to be Ukrainian in order to augment her credibility. Allen and Unwin, Darville's publisher, confirmed that the novelist "had made some stupid mistakes," but argued that "we still have a book of great power, a book daring to deal with awesome topics." Dershowitz's objections went largely unaddressed. But after the exposure of Demidenko as Darville, the threat of lawsuit was quietly withdrawn.

A more ambiguous instance of novelistic impersonation occurred in Ecuador, where Salomon Isacovici, a Romanian-born survivor of the camps, set out to tell his experiences under the German terror. He enlisted the help—and the Spanish language facility—of Juan Manuel Rodriguez, a Jesuit and former priest; it is not clear whether Rodriguez was amanuensis, ghost, or coauthor. In 1990, the manuscript, entitled *Man of Ashes*, was published in Mexico under both names and promoted as "cruel and truthful testimony of the Nazi concentration camps." Mexico's Jewish community praised it as a genuine work of witness and awarded it a prize. Isacovici died early in 1998, but three years before he had announced in a letter that he was "the legitimate author," that *Man of Ashes* was his autobiography, and that Rodriguez was hired only to assist with "the literary and structural parts of the book." Reporting in *The Forward*, Ilan Stavans, a writer and editor educated in Mexico, quotes Rodriguez as claiming that he "wrote the entire book, its title included, in six months, based upon [Isacovici's] manuscript and mutual conversations."

Rodriguez continues to insist that *Man of Ashes* is not Isacovici's memoir, but is, rather, the product of his own literary imagination. "I transposed many of my philosophical views to Salomon," he told Stavans. "My philosophical formation helped achieve the transplant and succeeded in turning the book from a simple account to a novel of ideas." The University of Nebraska Press plans to issue the book in English as Isacovici's memoir, with Rodriguez named as coauthor, and Rodriguez is considering a suit. "Salomon is my novel's protagonist, I am his author," he states. "I invented passages and details, and afterward he believed he had lived through them. For him the book is autobiography; for me it is a charming novel." Quite aside from "charming" as a description of Holocaust suffering, how may we regard what appears to be an act of usurpation? When Rodriguez declares a narrative of survival to be fiction, is the Holocaust being denied? Or is it being affirmed in terms of art?

The same query, steeped in similar murk, can be applied to the extraordinary history of *Fragments: Memories of a Wartime Childhood*, published as the memoir of Binjamin Wilkomirski, a self-declared Latvian Jew. The book, brought out by Germany's Suhrkamp Verlag in

1995 and by New York's Schocken Books in 1996, purported to be the therapy-induced recovered memory of a boy, born in Riga, who was deported at the age of three to Maidanek, a camp in Poland. Lauded as a literary masterpiece, *Fragments* won the Prix Mémoire de la Shoah in France, the Jewish Quarterly Literary Prize in Britain, and a National Jewish Book Award in the United States. It was endorsed by the United States Holocaust Memorial Museum in Washington, translated into more than a dozen languages, and eloquently blurbed by established writers. Its success leant credence to the theory that profoundly repressed memory, even of events very early in life, can be retrieved; and it also offered, in a child's pure voice, a narrative of German oppression to set beside the classic accounts of Elie Wiesel and Anne Frank.

All this began to disintegrate when Daniel Ganzfried, a Swiss writer and the son of a Holocaust survivor, undertook to verify Wilkomirski's assertions. He found, instead, inconsistencies of dates and facts, as well as documents identifying Wilkomirski as the child, born in Switzerland in 1941, of an unwed Swiss Protestant woman named Yvonne Grosjean. He also uncovered legal papers proving Wilkomirski's adoption, under the name of Bruno Doesseker, by a middle-class Zurich family. These disclosures have caused uneasiness among Wilkomirski's several publishers, but so far none has been willing—at least publicly—to call him a fraud. Holocaust historians note that no child younger than seven would have been spared instant gassing—demurrals that were, however, not voiced during the period of rhapsodic prize-giving. One speculation that arose in Wilkomirski's defense (reminiscent of Rodriguez's charge against Isacovici) is that there was no hoax; Wilkomirski committed no fraud because he believes in his written story and takes it to be his own. Perhaps he does. In that event we might wish to dub him insane. Even so, his conviction, if conviction it is, has done harm: it led a survivor living in Israel to suppose that he had recovered his lost son, whom he had thought long dead.

There was more. Defending yet another award bestowed on Wilkomirski by the American Orthopsychiatric Association (and eschewing human bafflement), a psychologist who is a member of that organization stated: "We are honoring Mr. Wilkomirksi not as historians or politicians, but as mental-health professionals. What he has written is important clinically." From this it would be fair to conclude that "mental-health professionals" care nothing for historical evidence and do not recognize when they are, in fact, acting politically. If Mr. Wilkomirski is indeed a fabricator, then to laud him is to take a stand—politically—on the side of those who declare the Holocaust to be a fabrication. In any case, how does it advance the public cause of mental health to encourage a possible public liar who is possibly an opportunist and possibly a madman?

The conflict between the freedom to invent and an honest confrontation with the constraints of the historical record remains muddled—and, often enough, muddied. If the subject were, say, the Homeric wars, the muddle might be benign, even frolicsome, a simulacrum of trickster literature. But the subject is the Holocaust, and the issue is probable fraud, hoax, or delusion. What is permissible to the playfully ingenious author of *Robinson Crusoe*—fiction masking as chronicle—is not permitted to those who touch on the destruction of six million souls and on the extirpation of their millennial civilization in Europe.

Yet the question of the uses of the imagination does not and cannot stop even here. Beyond the acrobatics of impersonation, or the nervy fakery of usurpation, lies a sacred zone consecrated to the power of art: or call it, more modestly, literature's elastic license. I have in mind two novels, *Sophie's Choice*, by William Styron, and *The Reader*, by Bernhard Schlink—one first brought out in 1979, the other published in 1997; one long acclaimed, the work of a contemporary American literary master, the other by a highly praised German writer. Both novels clearly intend to attach their stories to the actuality of the death camps.

Sophie's Choice followed by a dozen years Styron's Pulitzer Prize–winning *Confessions of Nat Turner*, and, like the latter, became a celebrated best-seller. Opening as a richly literary Bildungsroman, it recounts the often charming fortunes of Stingo, a young and untried Southern writer whose attraction to New York lands him in Brooklyn, "the Kingdom of the Jews." In Mrs. Yetta Zimmerman's rooming house Stingo meets Nathan Landau and his lover, a beautiful Polish woman named Sophie. Nathan is Jewish and mad—a paranoid schizophrenic, erratic when lucid, brutal and suicidal otherwise. Sophie is tormented by a horrific past, which she discloses to Stingo, piecemeal, as the two halves of the novel, Brooklyn and Auschwitz, begin to converge. And it is on account of Sophie's Auschwitz tribulations that *Sophie's Choice* has had an enduring reputation as a "Holocaust novel."

There is some justification for this, at least for the well-researched historical sections dealing with the Final Solution in Poland. Primo Levi, in *The Drowned and the Saved*, affirms that 90 to 95 percent of the victims of Auschwitz were Jews, and Styron's factual passages do not depart from this observation. His information concerning Polish Christians in Auschwitz is far thinner; it is, in fact, nearly absent. He gives us Sophie herself, but fails to surround her with the kind of documentation that he supplies for the deportation of Jews: exact dates of arrival in Auschwitz, for instance, as when he recounts the gassing of a contingent of Greek Jews, or when he enumerates figures for the Jewish population of Warsaw before 1939, or when he notes that the "resettlement" from the Warsaw Ghetto took place in July and August of 1942. Wherever the fingerprint of Styron's Holocaust research appears—and it appears frequently and accurately—it points to Jews. When he turns to Polish Christians, he apprises us of the Nazis' *Lebensborn* project, which sent "Aryan"-looking Polish children to be reared as Germans in Germany; of the Polish resistance movements, many of them zealously anti-Semitic—though the two resistance workers featured in the novel are passionately concerned for Jews; of a boxcar filled with the corpses of Polish children rejected for *Lebensborn*; and of the rescinded plan to tattoo Polish Christian prisoners. Sophie's father and husband are depicted as serious Jew-haters. For the seventy-five thousand Polish Christians murdered in Auschwitz, Styron's novel provides no data, no detail; or, rather, Sophie alone is the detail. But seventy-five thousand Polish Christians *were* murdered in Auschwitz, and that is fact enough. If Styron's Auschwitz research leads voluminously to Jews, it is because the murdered Jews voluminously outnumbered the murdered Polish Christians; yet— incontrovertibly—the factory of inhumanity that was Auschwitz produced complete equality of unsurpassed human suffering. Here there can be no hierarchy, nor may suffering be measured in numbers, or by majorities, or by percentages.

Still, what does it signify—does it signify at all—that the author of *Sophie's Choice* chooses as his protagonist an inmate of Auschwitz who is a Polish Catholic? Here is a fictional decision that by no means contradicts a historical reality. It is the truth—but is it the whole truth, the representative truth? And again, under the rules of fiction, why must a writer's character be representative of a statistical norm? Under the rules of fiction, if Bovary is not typical of most French women, and if Karenina is not typical of most Russian women, why should William Styron's Sophie be representative of the preponderant female population of Auschwitz? What does the autonomy of the imagination owe to a demographic datum? Or ask instead, what does individual suffering owe to the norm? Will the identity of the norm dare to compromise or diminish or denigrate one woman's anguish?

Come now to Bernhard Schlink's *The Reader*, a novel by a practicing judge, a professor of law at the University of Berlin. Its narrator is a law student who is presented as a self-conscious member of the "second generation"—the children of those who were responsible for the Nazi regime. The narrative begins postwar, when an intellectual teenage boy, the future law student, strikes up an unexpected friendship with a streetcar conductor, a woman markedly older than himself. The disparate friends rapidly become lovers, and their affair takes on an unusual routine of added romantic pleasure: in scenes tender and picturesque, as in a Dutch interior, the boy reads aloud to the woman. Only many years later—the occasion is a war crimes trial—is the woman revealed as an illiterate. And as something else besides: she is a former SS guard in a camp dedicated to the murder of Jews. An unsuspecting youth in the arms of an unconfessed female Nazi: over this retrospective image falls, unavoidably, the shadow of what some call Nazi porn.

Contemplating the predicament of young Germans after their nation's defeat, the narrator asks, "What should our second generation have done, what should it do with the knowledge of the horrors of the extermination of the Jews? . . . Should we only fall silent in revulsion, shame, and guilt?" "Our parents," he explains, "had played a variety of roles in the Third Reich. Several among our fathers had been in the war, two or three of them as officers of the Wehrmacht and one as an officer of the Waffen SS. Some of them had held positions in the judiciary or local government. Our parents also included teachers and doctors and . . . a high official in the Ministry of the Interior."

In short, an educated generation. To the narrator's observations, let us add Goebbels, a novelist and playwright; Speer, an accomplished architect; and perhaps also Goering, an art collector—or looter—with a taste for masterpieces. None of this can surprise. Germany before the Second World War was known to have the most educated population in Europe, with the highest standard of literacy. Yet the plot of Schlink's narrative turns not on the literacy that was overwhelmingly typical of Germany, but rather on an anomalous case of illiteracy, which the novel itself recognizes as freakish.

And this freakishness is Schlink's premise and his novel's engine: an unlettered woman who, because she could not read a paper offering her a job in a factory, passed up the chance and was sent instead to serve in a brutal camp. After the war, when she is brought to trial, the narrator acknowledges that she is guilty of despicable crimes—but he also believes that her illiteracy can, to a degree, mitigate her guilt. Had she been able to read, she would have been a factory worker, not an agent of murder. Her crimes are illiteracy's accident. Illiteracy is her exculpation.

Again the fictive imagination presses its question: is the novelist obligated to represent typicality? If virtually universal literacy was the German reality, how can a novel, under the rules of fiction, be faulted for choosing what is atypical? The novelist is neither sociologist nor journalist nor demographer nor reality-imitator, and never mind that the grotesquely atypical turns out to be, in this work by a member of the shamed and remorseful second generation, a means of exculpation. Characters come as they will, in whatever form, one by one; and the rights of imagination are not the rights of history. A work of fiction, by definition, cannot betray history. Nor must a novel be expected to perform like a camera.

If there is any answer at all to this argument (and the argument has force), it must lie in the novelist's intention. Intention is almost always a private, or perhaps a secret, affair, and we may never have access to it. Besides, the writer's motivation does not always reveal itself even to the writer. It would seem, though, that when a novel comes to us with the claim that it is directed consciously toward history, that the divide between history and the imagination is being purposefully bridged, that the bridging is the very point, and that the design of the novel is to put human flesh on historical notation, then the argument for fictional autonomy collapses, and the rights of history can begin to urge their own force. The investigation of motive is history's task, and here a suspicion emerges: that Sophie in Styron's novel was not conceived as a free fictional happenstance, but as an inscribed symbolic figure, perhaps intended to displace a more commonly perceived symbolic figure—Anne Frank, let us say; and that the unlettered woman in Schlink's novel is the product, conscious or not, of a desire to divert from the culpability of a normally educated population in a nation famed for *Kultur.*

Everything the camera has guilelessly shown—the burning of Jewish houses of worship, the burning of Jewish books, the humiliation of Jewish fathers, the terrorization of Jewish children, the ditches heaped with Jewish dead—touches on the fate of Jews in twentieth-century Europe. The pictures are fixed. In the less stable realm of words, the ghastly syllables of "Auschwitz" have resolutely come to denote the intent—and the means—to wipe out every last living Jew, from newborn infants to the moribund elderly in nursing homes. It is sometimes forgotten that the Nuremberg Laws and the Final Solution—the fundamental initiating elements of the Holocaust—were directed at Jews and only at Jews. In a speech in January 1939, Hitler looked forward to "the annihilation [*Vernichtung*] of the Jewish race in Europe"; nothing could be more explicit, and this explicitness succeeded in destroying one-third of the world's total Jewish population.

But the Holocaust is defined by more than the destruction of lives. German national zeal under Nazism exacted an abundance of victims, the Poles painfully and prominently among them. Let us make no mistake about this, and let us not minimize any people's suffering. Eleven million human beings met their deaths during the Nazi period; yet not all eleven million were subject to the Final Solution. The murderous furies of anti-Semitism and the wounds of conquest and war, however lethal, cannot be equated. The invasion and occupation of Poland were deeply cruel; but the Holocaust is not about the invasion and occupation of one nation by another. There is a difference between the brutal seizure of a country (Poland, Czechoslovakia, Holland, and so forth) and the achieved extirpation of an entire civilization. In the aftermath of the German occupation, Polish land, language, and Church were still extant. What defines the Holocaust is not the murders alone, but their irreversible corollary: the complete erasure of Jewish academies, libraries, social and religious bodies—the whole vast and ancient organism, spiritual and intellectual, of European Jewish civilization.

Auschwitz is that civilization's graveyard (a graveyard lacking the humanity even of graves); and herein lies the inmost meaning of the ideology of the death camp. Auschwitz represents the end not simply of Jewish society and culture, but of the European Jewish soul. Then how is it possible for a writer to set forth as a purposeful embodiment of Auschwitz anything other than the incised, the historically undisputed, principle and incarnation of the Final Solution? The German occupation of Poland enslaved, abused, murdered; it was a foul evil; it merits its own distinct history and commemoration. But it was not the Final Solution. The attempt to link the two—the annihilation of all traces of Jewish civilization with Poland's fate under Nazi rule—is to dilute and to obscure, and ultimately to expunge, the real nature of the Holocaust.

Sophie, then, is not so much an individual as she is a counter-individual. She is not so much a character in a novel as she is a softly polemical device to distract us from the epitome. The faith and culture of Catholic Poles were not the faith and culture targeted by the explicit dogmas of the German scheme of *Vernichtung*. Styron's Sophie deflects from the total rupture of Jewish cultural presence in a Poland that continues with its religion and institutions intact.

And when a writer describes in his novel the generation complicit in Jewish genocide as rife with members of the judiciary, physicians, lawyers, teachers, government officials, army officers, and so on, what are we to think when he fabricates a tale of German brutality premised on the pitiful absence of the alphabet? Who would not pity the helplessness of an illiterate, even when she belongs to the criminal SS? And have we ever before, in or out of fiction, been asked to pity a direct accomplice to Nazi murder? Here again is a softly rhetorical work that deflects from the epitome. It was not the illiterates of Germany who ordered the burning of books.

In the name of the autonomous rights of fiction, in the name of the sublime rights of the imagination, anomaly sweeps away memory; anomaly displaces history. In the beginning was not the word, but the camera—and at that time, in that place, the camera did not mislead. It saw what was there to see. The word came later, and in some instances it came not to illumine but to corrupt.

Memory and Memoirs

2

Do Facts Matter in Holocaust Memoirs? Wilkomirski/Wiesel

SUSAN RUBIN SULEIMAN

THE FRENCH POET André Breton once wrote, "Life is other than what one writes" (1960, 27). He did not mean that writing is a lie, but rather that writing is always one step behind or ahead of or next to the facts of lived experience—all the more so when that experience took place decades ago. This essay will attempt to follow up on some of the theoretical implications of Breton's remark.[1] What happens to the gap between facts and writing when the latter is concerned with issues of great collective significance such as the Holocaust? The two examples I will discuss—Binjamin Wilkomirski's *Fragments* (1996) and Elie Wiesel's *All Rivers Run to the Sea* (1995)—both raise, albeit in very different ways, questions about memory and its relation to historical truth. Having been published as literary memoirs, they also raise questions about genre. In what *kind* of writing do facts matter most, and why?

"Memory" and "memoir" are almost the same word in English,

---

1. An earlier version of this essay was published in *Poetics Today* 21, no. 3 (Fall 2000). I wish to thank Meir Sternberg and Marianne Hirsch for their scrupulous readings of the first draft and their useful suggestions for revision.

and are the same word in French: *mémoire*. But memory is a mental faculty, while memoir is a text. Although memoirs have no specific formal characteristics (other than those of autobiographical writing in general, which comes in many varieties), they all have at least one thing in common: a memoir gives "an account of the personal experiences of an author."[2] Unlike a full-scale autobiography, a memoir can be confined to a single event or a single moment in a life. It need not be the work of an important person, nor does it have to be well written (though that helps). Its primary claim to our attention is not literariness, but factuality. In the novelist Anna Quindlen's words, "What really happened—that is the allure of memoir" (1997, 35). She adds almost immediately, however: "Fact is different from truth, and truth is different from insight . . . [W]ith few exceptions, . . . fiction tells the truth far better than personal experience does" (1997, 35).

It may seem that Quindlen is suggesting fiction has no relation to personal experience, but her argument is just the opposite: personal experience, when written, veers almost inevitably toward fiction. The necessity for details that give the "feel of life" to narrated experience leads almost inevitably toward invention—which is why, as a former journalist who respects facts too much to invent them, Quindlen quips that she "will never write a memoir." In a more serious vein, she concludes: "I'm suspicious of memory itself . . . Memory is such a shapeshifter of a thing, so influenced by old photographs and old letters, self-image and self-doubt" (1997, 35). Individual memories may merge with family mythologies, eventually taking on the feel of lived recollection. Quindlen's essay reminds us,

---

2. This is the first definition given in *The American Heritage Dictionary of the English Language*, 4th ed.

in a pithy way, that the bedrock of factuality on which memoir rests (or is assumed to rest) is as fragile as memory itself.

Does that mean there are no significant differences between memoir and novel, between recollection and invention? No. Significant differences exist, but they are not so much textual as conventional or institutional. Textually, a fiction can imitate any kind of speech act, including the act of imperfectly recollecting a personal past. We have a brilliant demonstration of it in W. G. Sebald's novel *The Emigrants,* whose narrator recalls fragments of his own past and seeks out the stories of dead relatives and acquaintances as they are recalled, incompletely and imperfectly, by those who knew them. Sebald even includes photographs in the book, a fascinating insertion of "the real" into a novel—but these photographs, apparently of real people long ago, highlight rather than efface the ontological difference between their historical subjects and the fictional characters whose stories they ostensibly illustrate.[3]

In other words, novels can look and feel textually like memoirs. Is the opposite also true? One has but to look at the most successful memoir of the last few years, Frank McCourt's *Angela's Ashes,* to realize how close it is, *in its writing,* to a novel. Not only is McCourt's prose stylized, deploying a full range of rhetorical figures from anaphora to ellipsis to metaphor to onomatopoeia, but he also pres-

---

3. The question of fictional versus historical narrative is one of the oldest in literary theory, discussed both by Plato and Aristotle and by hundreds of theorists since then. For a concise and thorough recent overview of the various meanings attributed to the term "fiction," see Cohn 1999, chap. 1. Cohn's definition of fiction (following Paul Ricoeur's in his magisterial study *Temps et récit* [1983–85]) as "nonreferential narrative" is one I subscribe to, on the whole. I do not agree with Cohn, however, that fictional narrative is "ruled by formal patterns that are ruled out in all other orders of discourse" (p. vii).

ents us with detailed dialogues that took place before his and even before his mother's birth! No reader can be unaware of such literary artifice and patterning—and yes, invention—in this work; yet *Angela's Ashes* is internationally recognized as a memoir, recounting events that really happened during the author's impoverished childhood in New York and Limerick.[4]

Textual traits, then, do not necessarily provide a criterion for distinguishing memoirs from novels written in the first person: the two genres look alike.[5] Yet the first question that any reader asks about a written narrative is: "Is it fiction or nonfiction?" And the way the work is read will largely be determined by the answer to that question. (Here as in some other domains, one finds parallels between genre and gender: despite psychological and biological demonstrations of the difficulty in drawing absolute lines between the sexes, the first question we still ask about a newborn child is: boy or girl?) There exists a conventional, institutional boundary between a work

---

4. McCourt has recounted in interviews that travel tours are being organized to visit the sites in Limerick immortalized in his memoir. This fact bears out the referential appeal of his book—but just to complicate matters, in St. Petersburg, tourists can visit both the house where Dostoevsky wrote *Crime and Punishment* and, in the same neighborhood, the house where his fictional creation Raskolnikov killed the old pawnbroker. . . . (One interview where McCourt describes the Limerick tours appeared in a Swiss paper, *Sonntagszeitung*, September 9, 1998).

5. Narratologists, following the lead of Philippe Lejeune's classic work on autobiography, *Le pacte autobiographique* (1975), propose a single decisive textual criterion: if the proper name of the narrator-protagonist is identical with that of the author on the book's cover, the work is autobiography, not fiction. But many works do not tell us the narrator's name, and some contemporary writers have taken pleasure in playing with the criterion itself—whence the genre that Serge Doubrovsky has dubbed "autofiction," where the narrator-hero's name is identical to the author's but the work is presented as a novel. A highly autobiographical novel, to be sure—see, for example, Doubrovsky 1989.

offered as memoir and a work offered as novel. Meir Sternberg, discussing the difference between fictional and historical narrative, puts it succinctly: "What kind of contract binds [writer and audience] together? What does the writer stand committed to? What is the audience supposed to assume?" (1985, 26). In Sternberg's view (one he shares with many other theorists), the most important distinction between the two modes is that historical writing makes truth claims, whereas fictional writing is independent of such claims.[6] This distinction is conventional, not textual (many novels begin with a statement such as "I'm going to tell you my true story"). By conventional, I mean the set of implicit and explicit understandings that frame the publication and reception of any work, starting with the contract between author and publisher, proceeding with critical reception, and ending with the placing of the work on bookshelves of libraries and bookstores—and, in the case of a lucky few, in the columns of the *New York Times* best-seller list.

Memoirs resemble historical narratives insofar as they make truth claims—more exactly, claims to referentiality and verifiability—that put them on the other side of a boundary from novels. Interestingly, this conventional boundary becomes most apparent when it is violated, in cases of fraud or hoax. (Fraud or hoax does not refer to memoirs that "don't tell the whole truth"—few memoirs do; it refers,

6. This view, expressed in varying terminologies, is shared by Cohn, Ricoeur, and others. Christopher Ricks, going one step further, argues that even in novels, factual accuracy about historical events, places, or people is important to the reading experience. Here one might want to invoke Sternberg's distinction between truth-claim and truth-value, the latter referring to factual *accuracy* (as opposed to "commitment"). For Ricks, factual inaccuracies mar the reader's experience even of a novel, especially a realist novel—assuming, of course, that the reader "catches" the inaccuracy. (See Ricks 1990; I thank Dr. John Silber for informing me about this essay.)

rather, to the work as a whole and its relation to the writer—this point will become clearer in a moment). Equally interestingly, the violation is felt as violation only in the direction from memoir to novel, not vice-versa. No one cares particularly—except perhaps the author's friends and family—if a work billed as an autobiographical novel turns out to be straight autobiography. But if a memoir is shown to be fraudulent, because the person who claims to be recounting his or her experiences couldn't possibly have had those experiences or anything like them, then shock waves are created. All the more so if the experiences recounted are traumatic, whether in the framework of an individual life as in memoirs of sexual abuse, or in the framework of collective experience as in memoirs about war or genocide.

This brings me to the current, by now widely discussed case of Binjamin Wilkomirski and his book *Fragments: Memories of a Wartime Childhood*. Received with nearly universally hyperbolic praise when it first appeared in Germany in 1995 and shortly thereafter in English and many other languages, *Fragments* presents itself as a memoir, specifically a Holocaust memoir written by a Jew who lived through horrendous experiences in extermination camps in Poland as a very young child.[7] The memoir won several awards in the United States and abroad; its author, a Swiss musician and instrument maker whose first book this was, appeared in numerous official venues and was the

---

7. Although some of the first reviewers (such as Robert Hanks in *The Independent* [1996]) mentioned the book's self-conscious artistry, others (e.g., Susannah Heschel in *Tikkun* [1997]) praised its absence of "artifice" and its "unpretentious recounting of a child's inner life." Jonathan Kozol, while aware of the book's "stunning and austerely written" quality, considered it "free from literary artifice of any kind at all" (Kozol 1996). The equation of "lack of artifice" with authenticity—and, conversely, of "artifice" with inauthenticity—is symptomatic of the factual appeal of memoir. "Artifice" in this context appears to mean "tampering with the facts" in order to achieve literary effects.

Do Facts Matter in Holocaust Memoirs? / 27

subject of documentaries and interviews as a child survivor of the Holocaust. The story he tells in *Fragments* is that, the sole survivor of his family, he was smuggled out of a Krakow orphanage after the war and deposited in a children's home in Switzerland, from where he was adopted by a childless couple. Enjoined by all the adults around him to "forget the past," Wilkomirski explains in an afterword that it took him many years to allow himself to speak or write about his memories. He likens himself to the hundreds of "children without identity" who survived the Holocaust "lacking any certain information about their origins . . . furnished with false names and often with false papers too" (1996, 154).

Fragments can be read as Wilkomirski's attempt to record the "shards of memory" that remained with him from his early childhood, and an attempt as well to show how those early memories continued to inflect his way of being in the world long after he had reached safety in Switzerland. Like *Angela's Ashes*, this is a highly stylized work: the decision to restrict the narrative perspective almost exclusively to the young boy allows for some very powerful effects. For example, when the boy first arrives in the Swiss home, he is left alone in the dining room, apparently just after the other children have had lunch. He is astonished to find that the tables have cloths and white plates, not the gray tin plates on bare wood that he is used to; when he goes closer, he is even more amazed: "The children hadn't eaten everything on their plates! They'd left bits in strips around the edges. These leftovers were all over everywhere, and apparently nobody was guarding them" (1996, 21). He rushes to the table and begins to stuff the cheese rinds—for that is what they are—into his mouth and clothes:

> These stupid kids! I thought.
> How can anyone be dumb enough to leave food lying around unprotected? They don't seem to have a clue. Maybe they're new

here, and they don't know yet that surviving means laying in supplies, finding a good hiding place, defending your food. Never ever leave food unguarded, that's what Jankl always told me. (22)

When the workers at the home discover the child with his mouth full of garbage, they are disgusted: "Cheese rinds! He's eating cheese rinds! Monster!" (23).

The clash of rules and worldviews between what the child had learned in order to survive in the camps and what he was expected to know in the "normal" world afterward structures this memoir, and is rendered with what can only be called a masterful artistry. Alternating between the boy's experiences during his first years in Switzerland and the earlier memories they trigger (for example, the view of baskets heaped with fresh bread on the breakfast table triggers his one memory of his mother, who gave him a piece of dry bread on her deathbed in Majdanek), the narrative moves forward and back, producing new experiences and new memories but no new understanding—until the final chapter, when the boy, already a senior in high school, discovers that the war really is over. Watching a documentary about the Nazi camps, he sees the liberation of Mauthausen by Allied troops, and realizes that he is free and that he missed his own liberation.

Fragments is a powerful book, as most of its first readers agreed. But it has been proved beyond doubt that it is a fabrication, the work of a man who is not who he says (and by all indications genuinely believes) he is. After more than a year of doubt and controversy following the first accusation of fraud in 1998, the German and American publishers withdrew the book from the market.[8] As the story now stands, Bruno Doesseker—for that was his legal name until he changed it to Wilkomirski—was indeed an adopted child,

---

8. See Carjaval 1999 and *New York Times* 1999. The book was published by Suhrkamp Verlag in Germany and by Schocken Books in the United States. The

but not one born in Latvia; rather, he was the illegitimate son of a Swiss woman, Yvonne Berthe Grosjean, who gave him up for adoption but kept sufficiently in touch with him to leave him a small inheritance when she died in 1981. Binjamin Wilkomirski is a "found" name, chosen by Bruno Doesseker/Grosjean when he became convinced of his "true identity" as a child survivor of the Holocaust. His powerful memoir is based not on his experiences, but on his fantasies and on the memories of others; before writing his book, Wilkomirski/Doesseker/Grosjean had read thousands of testimonies and historical works in his obsessive pursuit of a Holocaust identity.

This story, which reads like a psychological thriller, has already caused much ink to flow and will probably continue to do so for some time.[9] It is fascinating existentially, historically, and in terms of

---

first published accusation against Wilkomirski appeared in August 1998, in an article by the Swiss journalist Daniel Ganzfried (1998a), based on documents as well as interviews with people who had known Wilkomirski as a child. After replies by Wilkomirski (1998) and others, Ganzfried wrote two more articles in the same newspaper, repeating his charges (1998b, 1998c). The matter was complicated by the fact that Ganzfried himself had published, in 1995, a Holocaust novel based on his father's experiences. Wilkomirski continued vehemently to deny the charges; his publishers, as well as some specialists who had worked with child survivors or who had met Wilkomirski in person, continued to defend the status of his work as a memoir. Others, however—including the distinguished historian of the Holocaust Raoul Hilberg—claimed that from the start they had doubted the work's authenticity (see Lappin 1999, 48). The document that provoked the book's withdrawal was the report prepared by a historian, Stefan Maechler, who had been charged by Wilkomirski's literary agent with investigating the matter; his report was subsequently published (see Maechler 2001).

9. Aside from many articles in the European and American press, the most thorough and engaging accounts of the Wilkomirski/Doesseker story to date are by Elena Lappin (1999), Philip Gourevitch (1999), Stefan Maechler (2001), and Blake Eskin (2002).

narrative theory. Here I will focus only on two questions, relating to problems of factuality and of genre.

First, should we care whether *Fragments* is a memoir or a fabrication—does it matter, finally, who Wilkomirski is and what the generic status of his book is? I think it does matter, though perhaps not for the reasons that may immediately come to mind. I am not overly worried, for example, about the ammunition this book provides to the Holocaust deniers; the deniers have already had their say, in an article circulated on the Internet very soon after the story broke in 1998, "Des faussaires et des dupes" ("Of frauds and of dupes") by Serge Thion, a well-known French negationist and author of several negationist pamphlets.[10] Thion uses the familiar negationist device of reasoning by synecdoche: if a single detail in a testimony is false, that renders the whole thing false; if a single testimony is a fake, that renders all testimonies suspect. But we must resist such pernicious reasoning by association: if Wilkomirski invented his memories, it does not follow that Elie Wiesel or Rudolf Vrba (both of whom Thion mentions in his article) invented theirs.

Historians have never relied exclusively on survivor testimonies, and even less so on a single testimony, in writing the history of the Holocaust. This statement may seem obvious, but given the emotional stakes involved, it is worth emphasizing. It does not mean that history has a privileged access to "facts" whereas memoirs do not, merely that historians rely on multiple sources and confront various kinds of documents in constructing their versions of events. The constructedness of all narratives, including historical narratives, does not—as some people fear—undermine the historical existence

10. The sender of this Internet article (message dated October 10, 1998) gives its name as "Le Temps Irréparable," with the e-mail address tempus@flash.net.

of past events. Ernst van Alphen espouses what can be called a postmodernist view of Holocaust writing (including historiography), emphasizing the continuing reinterpretation and reframing of past events in the present, as well as the inseparability of event from interpretive framework even at the moment it is being experienced. But he insists, I think rightly, that the *existence* of the Holocaust does not depend on individual constructions: "If we are to make sense of the Holocaust, the ontological question of the reality of the event—did it happen—must be firmly distinguished from the epistemological question of how we gain access to it" (Van Alphen 1997, 64). To admit the constructedness of all narratives, including histories and memoirs, is not to renounce the distinction between invention and truth claim. Memoirs, in their own way, make truth claims: "This is what happened, to the best of my recollection." But even if every memoir about the Holocaust were to prove inaccurate in some details, that would still not negate the Holocaust's historical existence.

Positivist historians sometimes fall into the trap of reasoning like the deniers: Dori Laub recounts an anecdote about a survivor witness of the attempted Auschwitz uprising (October 7, 1944), who recalled her astonishment at the event but mistakenly remembered seeing four chimneys burning when in fact only one chimney had been on fire. According to Laub, the historians at a conference who watched the survivor's videotaped testimony concluded that all of it was unreliable: "Since the memory of the testifying woman turned out to be, in this way, fallible, one could not accept—nor give credence to—her whole account of the events. It was utterly important to remain accurate, lest the revisionists in history discredit everything" (Laub 1992, 59–60). The historians were no doubt right to insist on the documented facts about the uprising (which, it should be noted, are based in large part on survivor testimonies, by people who were more closely involved with the uprising).[11] However, the value—and the particular truth—of this survivor's testimony was not necessarily diminished by the error in factual detail. A psychoanalyst at the conference provided the interpretive frame: "The number [of chimneys set on fire] mattered less than the fact of the occurrence. The event itself [the uprising] was almost inconceivable. The woman testified to an event that broke the all-compelling frame of Auschwitz . . . That was historical truth" (Laub 1992, 60). At this point, we might want to differentiate historical truth from factual detail, or introduce distinctions between various kinds of historical truth. In either case, the woman's account is not discredited as testimony to the *existence* of the Auschwitz uprising.

To return to our question, then—Does the generic status of *Fragments* matter?—I believe the answer is that it does, but not because the existence of the Holocaust is at stake.[12] Nor do I think that if *Fragments* were a genuine memoir, that would guarantee the factual accuracy of every memory recounted in the book. A memoir, whether it be a Holocaust memoir or any other kind, provides only a single mediated perspective on reality, not a direct, immediate apprehension of the "thing itself." Theorists of narrative as well as specialists in Holocaust writing have amply shown that no first-person narrative is "untouched by figuration and by shaping" (Bernstein 1994, 47). To believe in "the absolute authority given to first person

---

11. For a detailed historical account, see Gilbert 1985, chap. 38. For indications of other sources besides survivor testimonies, see Czech 1990.

12. Obviously, subjects of huge collective importance magnify problems of factuality as well as of genre; it is because *Fragments* purports to be a Holocaust memoir that it has elicited so much attention—but its inauthenticity does not undermine the existence of the Holocaust, as some commentators have argued. For a further discussion about facts in memoir, concerning the Aubrac "affair" in France, see Suleiman 2006, chap. 2.

testimony," writes Michael-André Bernstein, is to give credence to "one of the most pervasive myths of our era" (1994, 47).[13]

I agree with Bernstein on that point. It does not imply, however, that categorical distinctions don't matter. Contemporary thought is fascinated by borderlines, those areas where boundaries begin to blur; but boundary blurrings can exist only because categories do. And of all the categories in our lives, those of fact and fiction, with their various literary equivalents such as memoir or novel, remain very strong—despite our theoretical sophistication about the constructed nature of representation, and even of perception.

Some contemporary writers play on those categories, mixing and twisting them in various ways; but such self-conscious playing does not do away with conventional designations—on the contrary, it maintains them. The French novelist Alain Robbe-Grillet includes in his autobiography (*Le miroir qui revient*) a character named Henri de Corinthe, who is clearly fictional. The autobiography still functions as autobiography, however, with some novelistic "nuggets" in it.[14] A more interestingly ambiguous case is Georges Perec's *W ou le souvenir d'enfance* (*W or The Memory of Childhood*), which consists of two parallel narratives told in alternating chapters: a science-fiction narrative about the island of W, which finally turns out to be an allegory of the Nazi death camps, and a memoir about Perec's childhood in wartime France. Although both narratives have first-person narrators, the fictional "I" and the autobiographical "I" are differentiated: the appearance of Perec's name is a clear textual indicator in the autobio-

---

13. Similar arguments have been made by Eakin (1985), Ezrahi (1996), and Young (1988) among others.

14. In the subsequent volumes of what became an autobiographical trilogy (Robbe-Grillet 1987, 1994), the fictional element became ever stronger and the mixing of genres more self-consciously explicit and thematized.

graphical sections, while the nonrealist mode of the science-fiction segments indicates fictional discourse. Because the book contains an equal number of chapters devoted to each, it could be said to be a hybrid. But I think it is more accurate to consider it a combination, with its component parts juxtaposed, rather than a hybrid that merges them. The overall effect of the work depends on this juxtaposition, with the reader constantly "shuttling" from one world to the other and wondering what the relation between them is.

Unlike Perec's and Robbe-Grillet's, Wilkomirski's book does not *play* with categories; —it obfuscates them, which is not the same thing. The problem with *Fragments*, as a text, is precisely that it does not recognize—or at any rate, does not admit—its own fictionality.

This point leads to my second question: Is the solution to the problem simply to relabel the work, move it from "memoir" to "novel"? Or does it, rather, belong in another category, that of the discredited or false memoir? Given the highly crafted nature of this work, one can well argue for keeping it in print under a new label as fiction.[15] But if we take Wilkomirski's own affirmed commitment to referentiality seriously, we must hesitate to call his book a novel. In his afterword (which was included in the book because the German publisher had received a letter denouncing it and had asked Wilkomirski for an explanation), Wilkomirski states that the official identity papers he possesses have "nothing to do with either the history of this century or my personal history" (154). In a newspaper interview given in September 1998, replying to Ganzfried's accusa-

---

15. Arthur Samuelson, the American publisher at Schocken, told Elena Lappin in early 1999: "It's only a fraud if you call it non-fiction. I would then reissue it, in the fiction category" (Lappin 1999, 49). In November 1999, however, when the book was withdrawn from the market, there was no mention of reissuing it as fiction—at least, not yet.

tions, Wilkomirski suggested that the official document was forged by Swiss authorities after the war, just as in the case of other "children without identity" (1998, 51). The *New York Times* reported that, even when he was confronted by the historian Stefan Maechler's report, which caused the German publisher to withdraw the book, the author "declared defiantly, 'I am Binjamin Wilkomirski'" (Carjaval 1999)

Using the criterion of truth claim, therefore, we must call *Fragments* not a novel but a false—or better, a deluded—memoir. The question is, what happens to such works once they have been uncovered? Lappin mentions an earlier Holocaust memoir that was subsequently shown to be fiction, Martin Gray's *For Those I Loved;* Gray's book is now cited "only on revisionist websites" (Lappin 1999, 49). It would seem that a false memoir does not, by virtue of its falsity, automatically convert into fiction. More often than not, it converts into oblivion.[16]

But there is a factor we have not sufficiently considered yet: whatever else it might claim to be, *Fragments* is a work of literary art, powerful in its effect. Does it deserve to fall into oblivion? Tzvetan Todorov, in an essay aptly titled "Fictions and Truths" (Fictions et vérités), tells a story that bears an uncanny resemblance to

16. Wilkomirski's case bears striking similarities to a cause célèbre of about a decade ago, concerning *The Education of Little Tree*, which was purportedly an autobiography by a Native American and was praised for its authenticity—but turned out instead to have been the work of a white supremacist. Henry Louis Gates, Jr., reflecting on the *Little Tree* case, cites other examples of fraudulent autobiographies, notably some nineteenth-century slave narratives, which proved to be an embarrassment to their first publishers and promoters. Gates argues that "authenticity" is a category easy to fake, and suggests that the difference between factual and fictional writing may be ultimately impossible to maintain (see Gates 1991). Even if all that is granted, I believe the categories continue to function.

Wilkomirski's, even though it happened almost three hundred years ago. A hugely popular book published in London in 1704 and immediately translated into French, *Description de l'île de Formose en Asie* claimed to be an eyewitness account by a native of the island who offered lurid descriptions of its cannibalistic religious practices, among other exotica. However, it turned out to be a fake: "Today we know with certainty that the *Description* is a fraud, that Psalmanazar [the author] was never in China and that his real name wasn't even Psalmanazar"—this could be about Wilkomirski! (Todorov 1991, 140). But there is a major difference, which Todorov invokes in concluding his discussion of this work: "As a piece of historical writing, Psalmanazar's *Description* deserves no respect, because it is a fake. As a piece of fiction, it does not command admiration, because it does not present itself as a fiction and because its author lacks eloquence" (141).[17]

Although Todorov lumps them together, self-designation and eloquence are independent categories. Wilkomirski's book, too, "does not present itself as a fiction," but its author does not lack eloquence. What then? Todorov answers this question by invoking a completely different oeuvre, written two hundred years before Psalmanazar's fake: Amerigo Vespucci's letters about his voyages to the New World, *Mundus novus* and *Quatuor navigatones*. Todorov shows that these accounts too had problems: they were clearly full of fabulation and may not even have been written by Vespucci—but they

---

17. My translations. Like Wilkomirski's book, Psalmanazar's *Description* was challenged even before it was published: members of the Royal Academy suspected him of fraud, but the book was published anyway and enjoyed several years of notoriety. The issue of Psalmanazar's identity was finally laid to rest by the author himself, in his *Memoirs* published after his death (1764). Of course, one may wonder about the reliability of this work as well.

Do Facts Matter in Holocaust Memoirs? / 37

were artful and compelling, and earned their presumed author (who really did travel in the New World, at least that much is certain) "a continent" named after him. If they offered few truths about "American reality," they did offer truths, by their very artfulness, about the "European imagination" of the time (158). Earlier, Todorov proposed a distinction between "vérité-adéquation," or truth corresponding to facts, and "vérité-dévoilement," truth that reveals or unveils—the latter being presumably a function of literary skill (132).

Might we salvage Wilkomirski's deluded memoir by treating it as a compelling piece of writing that "unveils" truths about the effects of the Holocaust on the contemporary imagination? Trauma, horror, a sense of absolute victimhood: it appears that the Holocaust has become, in today's Europe and America, the ultimate signifier of such torments, even for those who have no personal connection to that past event. James Young has written persuasively about Sylvia Plath's poetic identification with the "Holocaust Jew," and the ethical and interpretive problems it poses. Plath was criticized, by Irving Howe and other Jewish critics, for her use of the Holocaust as a metaphor for personal suffering; the incommensurability of the two terms was, they argued, a trivialization of that collective event. Young, while recognizing and even sharing that criticism, nevertheless concludes that "to remove the Holocaust from the realm of the imagination . . . is to risk excluding it altogether from public consciousness. . . . Better abused memory in this case, which might then be critically qualified, than no memory at all" (1988, 133).

Wilkomirski's book presents an extreme version of this problem, a literalization of Plath's metaphors as well as of her self-identification as a "Holocaust Jew." Being an extreme case, *Fragments* poses certain questions starkly: Where does literature end (or begin) and psychopathology begin (or end)? Where should the line be drawn—should the line be drawn?—between personal memory and imagined or "borrowed" memory? To whom does the memory of the Holocaust belong? The fact that *Fragments* raises these questions, powerfully, may be reason enough for its continued presence in our literary landscape—if not as a memoir (it is not that), and not as a novel (it is not that either, at least not yet), then at least as a "case."[18]

· · ·

Fake memoirs can be works of art and they can be instructive, but they leave a bad taste in the mouth, especially when they concern a subject as fraught with emotion and collective significance as the Holocaust. In short, they are depressing. I want to conclude by considering a passage from a memoir whose status is not in doubt, and which presents a quite different—one might say an exhilarating, rather than depressing—problem of memory and factuality concerning the Holocaust.

In his 1994 memoir, *Tous les fleuves vont à la mer* (*All Rivers Run to the Sea*, 1995—volume 1 of a two-volume work), Elie Wiesel recounts once again some of the events known to readers of his classic Holocaust memoir, *La nuit* (1958; *Night*, 1960). After a detailed account of his childhood and early adolescence (before deportation) that complements the more sketchy presentation in *Night*, Wiesel evokes anew the horrific train journey that took him and his family to Auschwitz, a journey he had already memorably described thirty

---

18. This is strikingly borne out by the current position of *Fragments* as an appendix in Stefan Maechler's *The Wilkomirski Affair*. Whereas the original memoir was withdrawn from the market, it has reappeared as a piece of evidence in the "affair," a radical reframing. As I have written in a review of Maechler's book (Suleiman 2001), this reframing alters the nature of the text: the words are the same, but the work is not.

years earlier. One long passage, worth quoting in full, is especially pertinent to the present discussion:

> That train journey is described in my very first testimony, but one point requires clarification—and it's a delicate one: it involves the erotic atmosphere that supposedly pervaded the wagon. In the French version, I say: "Freed from all social constraints, the young people gave themselves up openly to their instincts and, under the cover of night, coupled [*s'accouplaient*] in our midst, without paying attention to anyone, alone in the world. The others pretended not to see." The word "coupled" provoked raised eyebrows among puritanical readers, which is not too serious, as well as among old companions who were present on the journey, which is more so. I therefore checked the original version in Yiddish. There, the passage reads differently: "Because of the promiscuity, many instincts were awakened. Erotic instincts. Young boys and girls, under the cover of night, succumbed to their aroused senses . . ." In fact, these were timid contacts, hesitant caresses that never went beyond the limits of propriety. How could I have translated this into "coupling"? I don't know. Or yes, I do know. A misplaced shame? I was perhaps speaking about myself. I was speaking about my own desires, repressed until then. I was lying next to a woman. I felt the warmth of her body. For the first time in my life I could touch a woman. A few fluttering strokes at her arms and knees, without her knowing it. The rest belongs to fantasy.
>
> I remember. (108; my translation)

Aside from its complex temporality (the narrative shuttles between the present, the past of the event, and several moments in between: the writing of the Yiddish version, the writing of the French version, and the response of readers to the latter), this passage is fascinating because it offers an intricate gloss on the problem of "facts and writing," which turns out to be—in more ways than one—a problem of translation. What exactly did the euphemistically vague Yiddish phrase "succumbed to their aroused senses" refer to? If writing is a kind of translation (imperfect, approximative) of lived experience, then what was the experience, the observed and recalled "fact" that the Yiddish phrase translated? And how best to render it in French?

Wiesel's realization that he had mistranslated his own Yiddish text—in both senses, since the French translation eliminated the ambiguity of the Yiddish and also offered what he now realizes was an inaccurate rendition of what took place in the wagon "in fact"— leads to what is perhaps the most interesting moment of this text. For in trying to understand his error, Wiesel discovers a whole new meaning, and offers us a whole new version (yet another translation) of his experience in the wagon; this new version, rather than "correcting" the previous one, brings another twist to a complex negotiation between memory and forgetting, or more exactly repression. What the first version (in both Yiddish and French) had repressed was the adolescent boy's first contact with the body of a woman. "Succumbing to aroused senses," perhaps even "coupling," turn out to be fantasies (still more translations?) projected by the boy, repressed by the adult author of *La nuit*, but remembered and recounted by the author of the memoirs more than thirty years later.

Does this revised version of the "facts" efface or attenuate in any way the horror of that train journey to the Nazi extermination camp? Does it alter the categorical status of *Night* as a Holocaust memoir, or of Elie Wiesel as a reliable witness? Obviously not. Rather, the revised memory adds a new layer to both Elie Wiesel's and the reader's interpretations of a life-shattering experience, one that has the virtually endless potential to be reviewed and reinterpreted.

To complicate things even further, the above passage is missing from *All Rivers Run to the Sea* (1995), the English translation of *Tous les fleuves vont à la mer.* When I noticed this omission (in looking for the passage to quote in English), it shocked me, but I discovered the reason for it by checking a recent English edition of *Night*: the English translation (based on the French text, not on the longer Yiddish original) has modified the lurid French verb *s'accoupler*, "to couple," to a much softer one: "young people gave way openly to instinct, taking advantage of the darkness to *flirt* in our midst" (Wiesel 1982, 21). In *La nuit*, translating his own ambiguous Yiddish text ("succumbed to their aroused senses") into French, Wiesel had chosen—for reasons on which he speculates thirty years later—an explicitly sexual, transgressive word that eliminated the ambiguity. I surmised that by the time *Night* appeared, he had been taken to task by other witnesses; so, for the sake of exactitude, he corrected the sentence in English: the young people, giving way to their instincts, did not couple; they flirted. This correction functions as yet another mistranslation, albeit this time with a restrictive rather than an expansive effect: "flirted" lacks both the suggestive ambiguity of the Yiddish phrase and the shocking explicitness of the French verb.

Elie Wiesel recently explained that the first English edition of *Night* (1960) had the correct translation from the French (itself, as we have seen, a mistranslation), "coupled." It was only about fifteen years ago that, prompted indeed by a desire for exactitude, he asked the American publisher to modify the sentence.[19]

Will we ever know (and do we want to know?) exactly who touched whom in that wagon and how? Personally, I regret only that

---

19. Wiesel offered this explanation in response to my paper (an earlier version of this essay) delivered at the conference celebrating his seventieth birthday, "The Claims of Memory" (Boston Univ., Oct. 25–27, 1998). The modification in the English version probably occurred when *Night* came out in the present Bantam edition, which is read in many schools in the middle grades.

the passage from the French memoirs was omitted in *All Rivers Run to the Sea*.[20] I am glad that Wiesel never corrected the French text of *La nuit*, since his error (or what he subsequently saw as such) allowed an extraordinarily rich reflection to surface in the memoir written thirty years later. The lesson to be drawn, finally, may be this: If memory is a "shifting and many-layered thing," never reaching the bedrock one longs for, then the way around that problem is not to keep silent, nor to confine oneself to fiction, but (to borrow a phrase from James Young [1988]) to keep on writing and rewriting. Breton was right, life is not what one writes. But one may never get closer to it than that.

20. In a personal conversation (January 23, 1999), Elie Wiesel and Marion Wiesel (who is his translator) said they too now regretted the omission; but after thinking about it, I realize it has a certain poetic appropriateness, another in a series of "mistranslations" that may be emblematic of the process of writing.

3

The Advantages of Delay
A Psychological Perspective on Memoirs of Trauma

SHLOMO BREZNITZ

I OFTEN WONDER WHY it took me fifty years to sit down and write *Memory Fields*, the story of my childhood during the Holocaust (Breznitz 1993). While the urge to tell the story was always present, it was matched by a host of excuses to procrastinate. Two among those excuses warrant mentioning.

First, there was the fear of fabrication. The temptation to embellish the story is hard to resist at any time, but particularly for a young person. Being aware of this weakness, the scientist in me (I was trained as a psychologist) rebelled against the possibility of adulterating truth with fiction. I thus held off until years passed and I was no longer prone to such fabrication. This was the best way I could find to keep my narrative as objective as possible. But even delay in setting down my story could not guard against unconscious manipulations of the truth. For even now, after all these years of waiting, I cannot account for details that, while untrue, found their entry without my awareness, through the back door of memory manipulation. This fact was brought home to me when, to my surprise, I found that my sister Judith, who was a full participant in some of the events I wrote about, recalled them differently. Yet there were other events where no other participant is available to corroborate what took place. As there is no independent evidence to rely on, one's memory, for better or worse, is the only beacon. Delay in writing the memoir helped to filter out much that wasn't true, but it could not eliminate every false note.

There was, however, another major reason for delaying, one that relates to the story itself. There are "big stories" and "little stories," and in the context of the Holocaust mine is certainly a "very little story." Compared to the major dramas of other survivors, most of my own experiences were without doubt minor. Judith and I were put into a Catholic orphanage run by the Sisters of St. Vincent a few hours before our parents were deported to Auschwitz. There we spent about a year, in frequent fear of discovery, until the end of the war. We were hungry, but not starving; we were cold, but not freezing; we felt abandoned and alone, but still cherished the hope of our parents' return. Many Jewish children in Europe experienced much greater loss and suffering, and very few of us survived. The "big stories" had to be told first. Only much later could the more fortunate ones gently follow in their footsteps.

The "big stories" are difficult to read and almost impossible to comprehend. Elie Wiesel has said that "Those who were not there can't understand." Unfortunately, the reader's ability to understand goes hand in hand with his/her ability to empathize. Thus, oddly enough, it appears that the "small stories" are much closer to "the thousand natural shocks that flesh is heir to" and are often better equipped to evoke a deep personal resonance.

The psychological distinction between *semantic memory* and *episodic memory* could be helpful at this point of our analysis (see Tulving 1985). Semantic memory deals with knowledge and its relation to other types of knowledge. Thus, in the context of the Holocaust one can remember the names of the camps, the dates of certain events, and the numbers of children murdered. Such knowledge is abstract in nature and entirely universal. There is nothing personal about semantic memory.

Episodic memory, on the other hand, refers to information stored as a specific event in the history of the person himself/herself. As such, it has a specific location and context, often with rich sensory elements. The two types of memories are stored in different parts of the brain, as witnessed by amnesic patients who lose their episodic memories while retaining completely their ability to retrieve semantic information, or the other way around.

It is much easier to share semantic memories than episodic ones. The "big stories" can't be understood in episodic fashion, only as facts. For those who were not there, there are few or no sensory markers attached to these facts. In contrast, survivors have less interest in the abstract facts; for them the camp was "their camp" with "their tattooed number" and "their family" lost.

Having procrastinated for such a period, I was naturally looking for some advantages of waiting so long to write about this experience. Being well on in years, I found that I needed less courage to tell the truth about what happened, some of which was not very complimentary to myself. It is difficult to tell of experiences in which one did not respond as one would have liked. When I was younger I shied away from telling these stories because I worried what the listener or reader would think of me. As one gets older, however, the way one acted as a child matters less. The ego diminishes, and there is less need to present oneself exclusively in positive terms. In addition, I think that one actually gets pleasure from presenting a more truthful and balanced view of oneself. Wisdom and experience appear to be more important than self-aggrandizement.

The temporal distance from the experiences also made it easier to write a narrative that would allow the reader emotional distance from the material. This desire for distance might appear paradoxical. Wasn't it important for the reader to have empathy with the boy who had undergone such tribulation—losing a mother and father and enduring a number of years of great hardship? Empathy was not the main response I sought to arouse. I wanted to write *Memory Fields* in a way that would enable the reader to reflect, to consider the implications of what I had gone through. Powerful emotion makes such reflection difficult, or entirely impossible. I know that, personally, I am easily moved by what I read, and, after I finish reading a very moving book, all I remember is that it was very moving and little else. I wanted readers to remember more than that, more than their own passion. I was aware that to help the reader achieve the necessary distance, I would first have to attain it myself. This distancing could be accomplished only once time had passed and I was no longer in thrall to the events I wanted to recount.

The following passage from the memoir illustrates how I worked to create such distance:

> It is an afternoon, of course, and Sister C. enters, breathless.
>
> The Germans are already in the courtyard, and there is no time for anything complicated. She urges all the boys to leave immediately, and I am quickly pulled towards Hans's bed, in the middle of the room. She covers me with the large down comforter, adjusts the bed to hide my presence, and leaves. It is dark and I am having trouble breathing.
>
> My heart beats fast, and I need a lot of oxygen. The whole thing has happened too quickly, and I am still disoriented. In her haste, Sister C. put me facing the wrong way, and I can smell the pungent odor of dirty feet.
>
> A minute goes by, and just as I am becoming more relaxed, the door to the right opens with the kick of a boot, and the hunters enter. There are at least two of them, maybe three. They shout something in German, but their voices are muffled by the thick

comforter. Then I hear a female voice: Mother Superior? Sister C.? More German, and then the sound of boots kicking the beds, and an additional noise, such as may indicate the forceful removal of blankets. I freeze. I want to take a deep breath and hold it for as long as possible, but there is not enough air. The smell is oppressive, and I start to sweat. As the kicks come closer, I become preoccupied with absurd details: Why Hans's bed? Because it is in the middle? Or because his comforter is the largest? Or because he is German? And then some bigger questions: Where is Rudo? And Judith?

It is obvious that they are coming closer and will soon discover me. I am suddenly seized by an urge to remove the comforter and inhale the fresh air. It is useless, anyway, so why suffocate? Perhaps if I give myself up they will show me some mercy. Certainly more than if they find me hiding under the comforter. What a foolish thought; these are Germans. It is like hiding from Death itself. Can one hide from Death?

I am sure that if I had been older at the time and had known the Samarkand story, I would have thought about it right then, under Hans's comforter. Once I had heard it, it was forever at the ready to ensure that no illusion would be allowed to dwell in my mind longer than it took to recall the story's frightening simplicity: A man is strolling in the marketplace when he is suddenly accosted by Death making threatening gestures towards him. He runs in panic to his master and asks his advice. The master responds, "You must leave here immediately and go as far as Samarkand, so Death won't be able to find you." Shortly after the man leaves, the master meets Death on the street and complains about the threatening gestures, to which Death replies, "I was not threatening. I was only surprised to see him here, knowing that we have a meeting scheduled for tomorrow in Samarkand." (Breznitz 1993, 125–27)

If there are lessons to be learned they require reflection and not just emotional empathy. One way of achieving distance is by cutting the emotional tension at its peak and inserting some food for thought. This was the purpose of the Samarkand story. The story interrupts the flow and keeps the reader from dwelling on the immediate danger that the boy faced of being apprehended by the Germans. To be sure, the story, too, deals with the realm of life and death. It does not, moreover, end happily. But it shifts the ground from a personal tale of a boy caught up in the events of the Holocaust to a parable about the folly of trying to escape the death that fate has assigned to one. The reader is no longer caught up with the events as they unfold. Rather, he is compelled to reflect on their significance. To comprehend its message requires analysis rather than simply identification with the characters.

• • •

To delay for so long before setting down one's memories has, of course, its disadvantages as well. First and foremost are the numerous tricks that memory plays. Some of these tricks are obvious, such as direct tinkering with the stored information, whereby memory distorts what took place. Other tricks, however, are more devious. I wish to mention two of the more subtle ways in which memory alters itself over time.

The first relates to a distinction made in current psychological theory, namely, that between *implicit* and *explicit* memory (Squire et al. 1990). The main distinguishing feature between the two is awareness. Whereas explicit memory relates to data that we know as being stored in our brains, implicit memory affects us without our being necessarily conscious of its existence. Thus, when searching our minds for an answer to a direct question, we are utilizing explicit memory. On the other hand, when driving a bicycle we rely primarily on memory that is implicit. We balance ourselves on the bike effortlessly, but will find it difficult to talk about how we actually do it. Implicit memory appears to operate automatically and does not require deliberate attempts on the part of the person to memorize something.

But there's the rub, for by the same token we are unable to prevent the automatic entry of a thought, even an unbidden thought, into our minds. A smell, a melody, a movement of the hand, and one is again in Auschwitz. This is the stuff that obsessions are made of. This too is the texture of a posttraumatic stress disorder, so frequent among Holocaust survivors.

Such entries into a trauma-related state of mind can happen to us several times a day without our awareness. This frequency, however, does not preclude their emotional impact, which may linger for a while. Thus we may feel anxious without knowing why, or have the sudden urge to check to see if the children are safely sleeping in their beds. It is by virtue of such automatic entries that Holocaust-related memories often become an omnipresent companion that will stay with us forever.

Words are often the means through which ideas access entry. They mediate between potentially remote contexts by virtue of both connotation and denotation. There is no shortage of words that bring one directly back to the Holocaust experience. "Final solution" does it, even if it appears in the context of a harmless problem-solving exercise. So does "six million," even if it relates to dollars rather than people. The gallery of such loaded words and concepts is sufficiently big to ensure entries in the midst of the most mundane activity.

The problem is, that it is easier to enter the Holocaust state of mind than to exit from it. Once engulfed by its heavy presence, how can one deliberately stop thinking about it? There is no simple way to exit by an act of volition, in the same manner that one cannot stop worrying simply by intending to do so (Breznitz 1971). With some luck, we are sometimes able to distract our minds from the source of worry without being aware of our success. Any such awareness would of course take us right away to square one.

The difficulty of exits could be illustrated by posing the following question: "How should the visit to a Holocaust museum end?" Should it lead to the parking lot? What are the psychological implications of the switch from Auschwitz to the search for the car? Or the visit to the next museum? Or to a place where one can grab a sandwich? While entries alter memories through both overuse and dilution, exits do so retroactively, by mixing the holy with the profane. Such exits leak into the memory, polluting it beyond recognition.

The second point refers to the cost of telling the story itself. Consider having had a pleasant experience that we want to share with somebody. After having told the story once, we tend to remember better the way we told it than the way it actually happened. There are many reasons for this. First, the telling of the story took place more recently than the events that gave rise to the original memory. Second, the experience, once narrated, takes on a defined structure, something almost always lacking in the more chaotic domain of real-life experience. As such, the story that was told is much more easily accessible than the experience that preceded and occasioned it. As we repeat the rendition of our story several times, the experience on which the story is based gets hopelessly lost. Between reality and narrative, there is no contest.

Photographing a beautiful scene has a similar effect. Once we look at the photograph, the photographic image invariably starts to replace the visual memory of actually viewing the landscape. Again, the photograph can triumph—image can win out over reality— because it is more recent, more focused, and more structured.

. . .

Given these psychological premises, the advantages of delay are clear. It follows that memories that we want to preserve for a long time are better kept to oneself. (By the same token, a negative experience that we want to get rid of ought to be told and retold as often as possible.) *Once we frame it in a story, the memory becomes frozen forever.* It has become a permanent fixture, existing almost independently of the person with whom it originated. To freeze memory is perhaps too heavy a price to pay for the pleasure of telling a story. Our memories are all we have. They are all we are.

Memory, History, Ethics

4

Memory, History, and Ethics

JOHN SILBER

MEMORY, HISTORY, AND ETHICS do not stand on equally secure footings, for neither history nor ethics would be possible without memory. Without memory, we would live in a timeless present, an undifferentiated now, that specious moment between what was (but that being unremembered, cannot be known) and what may be (but has not yet revealed itself). Memory is a necessary condition for living in time. We recognize the central importance of memory by the horror of its absence.

Alzheimer's, that death in life, that sickness unto death—the pity of which, as Kierkegaard observed, is that the sufferer cannot die—has been vividly portrayed in Elie Wiesel's novel *The Forgotten*. Without memory and time, the knowledge of which is dependent on direct or reconstructed memory, history as an account of the past would be impossible. Without memory and time, there could be no intentions or actions or duties; hence, no ethics.

But this triad is incomplete, as Cynthia Ozick has pointed out. Imagination is also necessary. As Thomas Hobbes observed, "Imagination and memory are but one thing, which for divers considerations hath divers names" (Hobbes 1982, chapter 2). What we remember is in part what we imagine; imagination is necessary in order to give meaning to experience. Imagination and memory commingle, for each is necessary to the fulfillment of the other. Imagination is also needed to experience the future as the future, for we cannot remember the future, nor can we experience it directly. But through memory and imagination we can extend the present backward and forward beyond that specious now to achieve duration, the continuity of experience that enables us to hold in conscious suspension the past, the present, and the future. And in imagination we put ourselves in the place and point of view of others, an essential step in assessing the rightness or wrongness of our acts. It is the practice required by the Golden Rule or by Kant's categorical imperative.

We remember what we have experienced. But what we experience would lack dimension, definition, texture without imagination. In chapter 1 of this book, Cynthia Ozick speaks of the iconic photograph of the little boy in the cap, with his hands above his head, held hostage by forces of the Third Reich. We are not dealing with fact stripped clean of memory and imagination. Without memory, we would not recognize the boy as a boy, or the cap as a cap. Without imagination, we could not put ourselves in his position and look back through his eyes and experience to some lesser but nonetheless significant degree his terror in that moment. Pictures in themselves, without memory and imagination, are meaningless.

Can it be true that photographs are more objective than words? Photographs are meaningless until recognized and interpreted, and with interpretation thoughts and words are added. And photographs themselves have lost their authority in courts of law because of the ease with which they can be altered to create whatever special effects are desired. I will return to this issue later.

But let us go back to the beginning. Let us take, for example, an event relatively free of ideological contention: Pickett's charge on the third day of the battle of Gettysburg. On the fiftieth anniversary of the charge, a reunion was held at which veterans from both sides reenacted the event. As the ex-Confederates neared the crest of the hill, the Northerners rushed forward to embrace them. At the seventy-fifth anniversary, there were, astonishingly, a number of veterans present. Their memories structured the reenactment; their recall of the carnage overflowed in emotions of friendship and reconciliation.

But there are no longer live memories of Pickett's Charge. It is carried in the recorded memories of witnesses, in geography, and artifacts, including photographs on glass plates, undoctored and genuine. The memories of eyewitnesses have been preserved in their own letters and memoirs and in their oral reminiscences, written down by others. In addition there are reminiscences spoken and written by those repeating what eyewitnesses have said. And then there are the earliest attempts to write history.

But with each passing year the deposit of memory in witnesses diminishes; witnesses die or suffer the normal infirmities of recollection, in which recollection and imagination commingle to leave something less than accurate recall of events as they occurred. The difference in kind between what is only imagined and what is remembered is eroded if not entirely erased by many factors. In chapter 3 of this book, Shlomo Breznitz notes that talking or writing about memory can cause its erosion, for what is then remembered is supplanted by what was said or written. The human tendency toward self-aggrandizement can also distort, as can the simple elapse of time and the natural erosion of memory as we age, an erosion that may terminate in senility.

Finally that day comes when no memory remains because the last witness has passed beyond remembering. All that is left is a great deposit of artifacts, memoirs, letters, photographs, drawings, journalism, and history. History becomes the only productive area, for one must be a witness to write a memoir, and there must be something newsworthy if one is to write journalism.

Memory is further challenged by the gradual transformation of the nature of history in response to ideological fashion, to changes in historiography, to the rise of historians variously intelligent and more or less perverse, and to complex webs of contingency.

History necessarily replaces memory, and whether it deserves the name of history or of fiction depends on the extent to which history adequately reflects or is a meaningful substitute for the complex of artifacts, memoirs, and recollections noted already and provides an accurate assessment of their meaning.

But history is quite capable of offering accounts by which people, perhaps most people, acquire surrogate memories wildly at variance with what actually happened. Perhaps this is the basis for Elie Wiesel's dark saying that some things that happened weren't true. Otto Eisenschiml, chemist and amateur historian and an intellectual rogue, published a book in the 1930s arguing that U.S. Secretary of War Edwin M. Stanton had orchestrated Lincoln's assassination. Eisenschiml's account had a certain plausibility, because he went through the motions of proper historical procedures and skillfully made slight but useful falsifications of the evidence. He related, for example, that immediately after the assassination all telegraph communication between Washington and the rest of the world was cut off. He also related that although Stanton had sent warnings to close the various escape routes open to Booth, he did not close the route that Booth actually took through southern Maryland to Virginia. While Eisenschiml's book is full of evidence of this kind, none of it is strictly true. Although the commercial telegraph line to Baltimore did go out of service, the rest of the commercial telegraph service was available, as well as the highly developed military communication system. Stanton did not close the route through Maryland for the reason that there were neither telegraph lines nor troops in the area.

Professional historians ignored Eisenschiml's book, but it sold well and remained in print. It inspired a whole school of less-talented and less stable emulators, and by the 1960s the Lincoln assassination had become a cottage industry. There were forgers in the field producing documents, including photographs, to buttress Eisenschiml's thesis as well as other extravagances. Booth was said not to have been killed in 1865 but to have survived into the 1920s.

The result of all this is that Stanton, whose devotion to Lincoln was heroic, is seen by many as the sort of man who would be capable of conniving in the murder of the president. Eisenschiml and his followers have never been taken seriously by established historians, and the memory of what happened is on the whole well preserved in thousands of books written about Lincoln. Nevertheless, the notion that Lincoln was murdered by his subordinates is alive and well in the intellectual fever swamps.

But let us consider more recent and far more serious examples of the distortion of history. Consider the movies of Oliver Stone, who has never met a conspiracy theory he didn't like. He trashed our national memory of the Kennedy assassination for no better reason than to make money. Because of this man's abuse of his immense power—a kind of power that did not exist until our time—the public understanding of the Kennedy assassination is unlikely ever to deserve the name of history. Was he killed by Castro, by the Mafia, by many, or by the single man Oswald? Stone's film has salted the mine of history with too many nuggets of what only appears to be pure gold.

Or consider the case of the Disney Corporation and its film *Pocahontas*. Now, if the issue is how many fingers Mickey Mouse has, Disney, as his creator, is clearly the authority: we must accept that Mickey has three fingers and a thumb. But *Pocahontas* is presented as a film about Pocahontas, an historical person. It was to be expected, of course, that the film would sentimentalize the Indians in the fashion in currency ever since the discovery of the Noble Savage. But Disney took still more extraordinary liberties. Captain John Smith had dark hair and wore the beard customary in his time and place. Disney's John Smith is blond and clean-shaven, because, in the feeble and hackneyed imaginations of the film's creators, that is what leading men look like. A generation of Americans will grow up with a distorted understanding of what Smith looked like. What Mr. Eisner adds to the bottom line he subtracts from our history.

And when the film *Apollo 13* was released, think of the boost in credibility it gave to those who denied that there was ever a moon landing. *Apollo 13* has the appearance of objectivity even though all of the scenes in space and on the moon were photographed in a large studio. We see the spacecraft landing on the moon, astronauts emerging and springing up and down. These were all special effects created by the movie industry. None authentically records what actually happened on the moon, although they are faithful representations of those events. The successful simulation of an historic event revealed the film industry's ability to create apparently authentic images of fictional events.

While one can recognize the extraordinary historical accuracy of *Apollo 13*, down to the smallest details—provided one believes that contemporary TV and radio reports of the landing were authentic—the fact that *Apollo 13* was entirely fabricated *on earth* gives rise to the possibility, and hence the suspicion, that it was only on film that the moon landing ever took place. It raises the possibility that Walter

Cronkite's original broadcast, with blurred and snow-filled televised pictures of the moon landing, was simply the first crude attempt by television producers to create a false impression.

There is no way any longer to sustain the priority of pictures over words. Digital photography enables any computer hack, however untalented as a photographer, to create photographs that are total fabrications, while *Apollo 13* demonstrates the ability of the film industry to fabricate the illusion of an event so authentic in appearance that a totalitarian government could use this technology to create an historical event—an event that later historians might fully credit even after exercising full professional testing and judgment.

The history of the Spanish Civil War provides an example of historical revisionism that resulted in a more balanced account. The history of that war was for a generation written largely by historians highly sympathetic to Marxism and the leftist politics of the second Spanish Republic. An account of the war in every way superior to the originally accepted version is that given by Hugh Thomas in his magisterial work, several times updated, *The Spanish Civil War.* This book had the honor to be banned under Franco even though it exposed the orientation and illusions of the veterans of the Lincoln brigade. Fairly soon we will have arrived at the point where there is no deposit of memory left in witnesses and we may hope that eventually something like the Thomas account will come to be received as the true account, just as his demolition of the vaunted health system of Cuba under Castro is increasingly accepted. (The poet Armando Valladares, in *Against All Hope,* wrote movingly of the torture inflicted by Castro, but his eyewitness account has been largely obscured by the Castro apologists and those who wish to trade with Cuba in disregard of human rights violations.)

It is tempting to say that one person's revisionism is another person's discovery of the truth, but there are usually certain earmarks of false revisionism. Consider the two most striking examples of revisionism in our time: the thesis that the United States was almost entirely to blame for the Cold War, and the claim that the Holocaust did not happen and was invented by the Jews for their own sinister purposes. Each of these movements claimed to offer a more accurate understanding of history than the accepted version—that is, one claimed to provide for the origins of the Cold War and the other for the history of the Third Reich what Hugh Thomas did in fact provide for the Spanish Civil War.

But unlike Thomas, neither of these schools will bear much scrutiny. The Cold War revisionists are a more sophisticated lot than the Holocaust revisionists, and their tactics are superficially more plausible. The Holocaust revisionists are for the most part amateurs, and their manipulations of historical records are more obvious. They recently suffered a bruising defeat when the historian Deborah Lipstadt successfully defended a libel suit brought by the neo-Nazi revisionist pseudohistorian David Irving.

What the two schools have in common is an ideological program that drives their "research" and renders their conclusions necessary. The Cold War revisionists reflect the biases and agendas of apologists for Marxism, Stalinism, and communism, while the Holocaust deniers represent anti-Semitism at its extreme. They are revisers in the sense that Orwell's Winston Smith, working in the Ministry of Truth, was a reviser. The body of the facts must fit the Procrustean bed of ideology, and if "the facts" need to be "adjusted," well, so much the worse for the facts.

In September 2001, revisionism jumped into high gear before the ruins of the World Trade Center settled. The fever swamps of the Internet reverberated with claims that the attack had been carried out either by Israel or the United States. One preposterous story alleged that four thousand Jews who worked at the World Trade

Center had been warned not to come to work that Tuesday; another made a similar claim about senior management. Here we have the revisionist technique of simple fabrication, but other observers were hard at work manipulating real evidence. It was soon noticed that in the weeks just before the attacks there had been a great deal of suspicious short trading in the stocks of airlines, airline companies, and reinsurance companies. The inference was obvious: Osama bin Laden had used his ghastly insider's knowledge to profit from his intended crimes. The revisionists brushed this idea aside with the false claim that Islam prohibits investment. Although Islam does prohibit lending at interest, the purchase of shares in corporations is a model of the transactions allowed by the Koran—transactions in which the investor assumes potential risks.

In the weeks after the disaster, it did not seem likely that these crackpot theories would gain any traction. But Oliver Stone has not yet been heard from.

The importance of history is that it is a source for the creation of memory. It is, in fact, an adequate surrogate for memory. Its importance has never been put better than in Orwell's formulation in the motto of the Party: "Who controls the past controls the future; who controls the present controls the past." It is Elie Wiesel's greatness that with regard to the Holocaust he has left an imperishable deposit of memoir that will ensure that the history of the future will be witness to the truth. The importance of Wiesel's memoirs, books, and stories years from now is encapsulated in an ancient Chinese proverb: "The palest ink is better than the strongest memory." This reflection is true primarily because the mind that possesses the strongest memory is mortal. The ink endures beyond the life of the one who remembers precisely.

It is ethically imperative that history bear witness to the truth. While it is not the moral obligation of historians to claim a standpoint of absolute objectivity, it is their moral obligation to subordinate ideology and personal preference to evidence and arguments left to them by those who were witness to the events and by the complex web of inherited facts unaltered by manipulation.

What we must recognize once again is Immanuel Kant's insistence on the primacy of practical reason. Historical records and facts are not secure and cannot be relied upon apart from the moral integrity of those who examine them. Historians are duty bound never to salt the mine of history by the creation of ersatz facts introduced to fulfill their preconceived ideas. We shall always have to distinguish between those who study, speak, and write with integrity and those who do not, for neither life nor history comes to us like a movie with subtitles saying, "This is the true version." We have to search diligently for the truth, and the pursuit of truth has to be guided by ethics. That is, historians must faithfully observe those procedures of investigation, research, and interpretation by which one comes closest to the true account.

While the imagination is essential in the interpretation of the world about us, it is not a license to fabricate. And although I am in no position seriously to challenge the view that fiction writers need not be restrained by facts, I don't believe that to be true. One cannot write a novel about Napoleon as a general in the Second World War or in any war other than the Napoleonic Wars. One can put the name Napoleon on a general or a private in a war that Napoleon never fought, but the character would not be Napoleon. Christopher Ricks has argued persuasively, in "Literature and the Matter of Fact" (1990), that works of the imagination when they intersect history must observe scrupulously all the facts of history.

I believe Aristotle was right when he said poetry is more philosophical than history. He meant that poets—especially dramatists—offer a truer and wiser understanding of actions than is ever likely to be delivered by historians. Imagination informed by thought can reveal in the work of a mind of genius the true essence of a matter more effectively than the account of all but the very greatest historians. They share the gift of poetry. And this, I believe, is what Wiesel meant when he said, "Some things that never happened nevertheless are true."

◆ *Memory and the Persecutor* ◆

5

Reflections on the Papon Trial

JEFFREY MEHLMAN

OUR SUBJECT IS MEMORY, and I should like to complicate matters a bit by speaking about what some have regarded as a fiasco of memory gone militant, the trial of Maurice Papon for crimes against humanity. It was the longest criminal trial ever held in France, and came to an end, after ninety-five days before the Bordeaux Cour d'Assises, at the beginning of April 1998. Elie Wiesel was at one point expected as a witness, but chose not to go. He is quite eloquent on the reasons for that decision, and it is to be hoped that he will one day share them with his readership.[1]

There is a sense, of course, in which the very idea of such a trial is at odds with the claims of memory. After all, the purpose of a trial,

---

1. In conversation, in the fall of 1997, he imagined the use to which his testimony might be put by the defense: a crescendo of feigned shock and disbelief at Wiesel's presence despite the fact that he neither knew Papon nor had been in France during the war, culminating in the reading of passages from the author to the effect that he had no idea of what lay before him in Auschwitz before his arrival. And if Elie Wiesel had no idea in 1944, the defense might continue, what can the defendant have known in 1943? On the ninety-fourth day of the trial, Maître Jean-Marc Varaut, Papon's principal attorney, showed up in court with a copy of Wiesel's *Tous les fleuves vont à la mer*. See Conan 1998, 303.

however instructive, is to dispense justice and thereby close the books on a gaping injustice. But closing the books is the last thing anyone in the grips of the imperative or compulsion to remember would want to do.[2] This may be one reason the great memorialist of the genocide, Serge Klarsfeld, ended up doing his level best to sabotage the trial. (The other reason was an almost visceral inability to tolerate a presumption of innocence in the case of this particular defendant.)[3] But I anticipate my argument.

Let me first evoke the terms, stakes, and idiosyncrasies of what was billed as a trial of the Vichy regime in the person of its exemplary civil servant or *haut fonctionnaire*, Maurice Papon. It was the improbable trial of an eighty-seven-year-old man fifty-five years after the crimes he was alleged to have committed, a trial hobbled by frequent recesses because of the failing health of the accused. Papon had been the number 2 man at the prefecture in Bordeaux during the last two years of the German occupation. As such, he bore responsibility for services relating to the war, including Jewish affairs (which meant deportation as well as the "Aryanization" or expropriation of properties), and for that reason he was indicted for "complicity in murder, illegal arrest and sequestration," defined as crimes against humanity. (In fact French jurisprudence had been tinkering with its crimes-against-humanity provisions for years, attempting to custom-fit its categories to the three different cases of the Gestapo agent Klaus Barbie, the French militia thug Paul Touvier, and now the career bu-

---

2. Whence the doubts of Claude Lanzmann, the director of *Shoah*: "I believe profoundly that there is no statute of limitations on crimes against humanity, but to judge them today is paradoxically to implement just such a limitation, to close the books on them [y mettre un point final]" (Lanzmann 1998).

3. On Serge Klarsfeld's efforts to derail the trial, see, in particular, Finkielkraut 1998.

reaucrat Maurice Papon.[4] One of the more chilling comments heard in the courtroom was a remark made by a lawyer noting that he had no illusions about French magistrates. Under the Occupation, they did what Pétain wanted; now they would do what public opinion demanded; the key thing was to have Papon stand criminal trial.)[5]

There were 1,560 Jews dispatched from Bordeaux to Drancy, the French camp northeast of Paris that was a way station to Auschwitz. Now the scandal of the crime of which Papon stood accused was interestingly complicated by a series of other scandals.

The first concerned the fact that Papon, as of 1943, had significant contacts with the Gaullist resistance (although he would not receive his membership card until 1958). This fact raised the question of how one might make the transition so swiftly from Collaboration to Resistance, from Pétain to de Gaulle, as well as what the opposition between the two might be if that transition might be effected so smoothly.

The second scandal concerned the extraordinary success Papon enjoyed after the war as an *haut fonctionnaire*. He was police prefect of Paris under de Gaulle from 1958 to 1967 and later minister of the budget under Giscard d'Estaing. Now as police prefect he was responsible for two particularly egregious episodes of police violence

---

4. See Conan 1997a. The French, out of fear that such a statute might be turned against French excesses in Algeria, have insisted on a definition in terms of crimes committed "in the name of a State practicing a policy of ideological hegemony." This definition worked for Klaus Barbie, but resulted in the case against Touvier, who had taken the initiative in a series of murders, being thrown out of the Cour de Cassation on April 13, 1992. Additional tinkering was required to convict Touvier. Finally, in order to try Papon, the same court determined on January 23, 1997, that an "accomplice in a crime against humanity need not adhere to the policy of ideological hegemony of the principal culprits."

5. See Conan 1997a.

against demonstrators for Algerian independence: numerous bodies were fished out of the Seine following the police action of October 17, 1961, which has frequently been called a massacre. Question: what relation might there be between Papon's role in the massacre under Pétain and Papon's role in the massacre under de Gaulle?[6] (At this point the Gaullists explode: might the whole purpose of the trial not be to discredit de Gaulle and the Gaullists, now seen to be, in the long run, of a piece with their wartime adversaries? Massive objections on the right.)[7]

Finally, the third scandal had to do with the extraordinary delay of the trial. The deportation orders bearing Papon's signature had been unearthed in 1981. Why did the trial begin only in 1997? There is no doubt that François Mitterrand, whose wartime career was not dissimilar to Papon's, played an important role in the delay. There is even a letter from Papon to Mitterrand of October 21, 1991, in which Papon all but threatens the president of the Republic with blackmail should he be brought to trial.[8] But there is also the fact that there were other candidates for prosecution, far bigger fish,

---

6. On Papon's role in the massacre of 1961, see Jean-Luc Einaudi (1991), *La Bataille*, as well as Einaudi (1997), "Les mensonges de Maurice Papon." Papon lost his suit against Einaudi for "defamation of a government functionary" before the Seventeenth Correctional Chamber of Paris in late March 1999.

7. Philippe Seguin, president of the Gaullist party Ralliement pour la République, denounced the secret "trial within the trial"—that of de Gaulle and the Gaullists. See Conan 1998, 37. The net effect of the trial, Seguin predicted, would be to swell the ranks of the Front National. See Chambraud, "Philippe Seguin."

8. See Conan 1997b. In that letter, Papon demanded "the right to be tried in criminal court, before and by the French people, and to confound in its presence both *those who truly adhered to the ideology of Vichy* and those who, using me as a vehicle, want to vilify the State and the nation" (my emphasis). On Mitterrand's Vichy career, see Péan 1994.

waiting trial before Papon—and who were now dead.[9] At least two lawyers for the prosecution had gone on the record in previous years against prosecuting Papon.

. . .

The delay in bringing Papon to justice is also crucially related to the history of French perceptions—or memories—of the war. These perceptions may be divided into two periods or phases, although I believe the Papon trial may mark the beginning of a third. Each period or phase of memory might be defined in terms of what it perceives as the crucial turning point in the evolution of the Vichy regime.

For the first period, which runs from the end of the war to about 1970, the turning point in the French experience of the war is November 11, 1942. The Allies invade North Africa; the Germans cross the line of demarcation and occupy the whole of France, and Pétain, instead of heading off to join the Allies in Algeria, gives the lie to the waiting game he claimed to be playing and stays put. It is at this point that the Vichy regime emerges as discredited, and the United States, for instance, which had backed Pétain over de Gaulle consistently, sees fit to set up a concentration camp, an admittedly luxurious concentration camp, for Vichy diplomatic personnel in Hershey, Pennsylvania.[10]

The second phase of memory, whose dominance begins about 1970, concerns a second turning point: the French-German agreements—the so-called Bousquet-Oberg accords—of June 1942. In a word, the French police offer to take a leadership role

9. Of these, the most notorious was René Bousquet, who was gunned down in his apartment by Christian Didier, a deranged writer, on June 8, 1993.

10. On the Hershey "concentration camp," see the memoir of Vichy's ambassador to the United States (Henri-Haye 1972, 316–21).

in the implementation of Jewish policy. Why? Less out of anti-Semitism, it appears, than out of a desire to maintain some measure of administrative autonomy during a time of foreign occupation.[11] Such pretensions to autonomy had already begun in October 1940 with Vichy's rush to pass its own anti-Jewish laws, which one historian calls a kind of French "apartheid."[12] And they progressed to the accords of the summer of 1942, whereby French policemen assumed principal (and even sole) responsibility for the massive roundup of *foreign* Jews facing deportation. However horrific, Laval's slogan of the time should not be forgotten: "The best way to save a French Jew is to turn in a stateless Jew!"[13] For all its dire consequences, we can not even characterize the slogan as anti-Semitic.

Two different perceptions of the war, then, pivoting on two distinct turning points. The first is alive above all to the question of dealing with the enemy and the "spiral of vassalization," as one historian puts it, to which it led.[14] The second is alive above all to the entry of the French State on the path of mass murder. It is that second perspective that has dominated, indeed obsessed the current generation, which the historian Pierre Nora has gone so far as to call the "Bousquet generation."[15] (René Bousquet, the man who cut the

---

11. See the testimony of Robert Paxton as reported in Dumay 1997a: "negotiating 'more responsibilities' for the police and the administration: 'that was the fatal mechanism . . .'"

12. See the testimony at the trial of Jean-Pierre Azéma, as reported in Dumay 1997b: "If the German conception of the world was racial . . . Vichy's was not. The Jewish question was not central. It was a portfolio among others. Apartheid and segregation, yes; extermination, no."

13. Laval regularly instructed prefects: "Every foreign Jew who leaves French territory is a French Jew that is saved" (Ferro 1987, 410).

14. See Dumay 1997c.

15. See interview with Pierre Nora (Nora 1997).

deal with the Nazis, the intimate friend of François Mitterrand, a friendship over which Elie Wiesel broke, if I read him well, with the French President.)

Why the shift? Or better yet, why did the genocide not loom as central to French perceptions of the war until 1970? Well, the first point to be made is that in the wake of the war, the right to forget, to put the camps behind one, loomed as large for many Jews in particular as the putative claims of memory. The tragedy of the Jews in France is that they had been separated from the rest of the nation. Was it not simple humanity that dictated that that separation not be rehearsed by the victors? So talk of the deported referred for the most part to resistance fighters, among whom the Jews were allowed to take their place.

And then, around 1969, the question of the deportation of the Jews, French anti-Semitism, and specifically French complicity in the genocide emerged as a French national obsession.[16] Why? Let me try two explanations. The most perverse explanation to gain currency in France runs as follows: In May 1968, French students arrived at the gates of the Renault factory in Billancourt with the pretense of handing the banner of revolution to their comrades at Renault. They were in short order dismissed, rebuffed: the proletariat claimed that it knew how to recognize class enemies and provocateurs when it saw them. The result was traumatic for the intellectual left in France, who then and there decided that it would be their generation's project to blacken the name of French populist sentiment, which meant, among other things, rewriting the French history of World War II as though the French population itself had been massively collaborationist and indeed anti-Semitic.[17] It is in

16. See Rousso 1991.
17. See Yonnet 1993, 232–53.

that context that Pierre Nora—original name: Aron—could speak of the current generation as the "Bousquet generation."[18]

A second explanation for the almost obsessive concern with French anti-Semitism since 1970, the somewhat suspect repetitiveness with which the French exclaim their shock every few months at revelation after revelation of French complicity in the genocide: I'm tempted to call it traumatophilia.[19] I take my clue here from George Steiner, for whom, one occasionally has the sense, if one was not present at the genocide, *on one side or the other,* one simply doesn't have the moral seniority to be taken seriously.[20] Just so: as France has come to weigh less and less in the balance of things, above all since the unification of Germany, it is as though the French were deriving a perverse satisfaction at being able to proclaim that they were there, crucially there, in what was after all *the* event of the twentieth century. "We were there, and in the rigor of some of our juridical stipulations, more there than the Germans themselves; therefore we exist." Thus would run the new French *cogito.*

Turn now to the Papon trial: the defense was based on the logical proposition that the best way to resist the Germans was to *feign* collaboration.[21] It is an attractive proposition in some ways. To sabotage from within is arguably more effective than to strike a purist pose

---

18. It has been widely observed that Yonnet's volume was published in a series directed by Pierre Nora, the influential editor of the *Lieux de mémoire* project at Gallimard.

19. I have developed this perspective in "L'Ombre de Vichy sur la littérature française: Entretien avec Jeffrey Mehlman" (Delacampagne 1994).

20. Such is the impression exuded by his remarkable novella *The Portage to San Cristóbal of A. H.* (Steiner 1981).

21. See, for example, Papon's statement to the effect that "the administration constituted the sole rampart of the population against the Occupant," in Conan 1998, 311.

from without. If Papon's argument were valid, however, it would mean that French national honor, in the best of cases, would be coextensive with French hypocrisy—a ticklish proposition indeed. Moreover, there was a counter-proposition: true, feigned collaboration might be the subtlest ruse of resistance, but might not feigned resistance, given French popular sentiment, be the subtlest ruse of collaboration? Example: Papon shows up at the Bordeaux train station with blankets and even travel upgrades for his Jews.[22] Nice guy, no need to fear, no incentive to riot: the deportation would be carried off all the more smoothly.[23]

Think then of the delicacy of the situation on which the trial, from a logical point of view, pivoted: if feigned collaboration is the subtlest ruse of resistance (and even de Gaulle from London had asked Vichy bureaucrats loyal to him to stay in their positions), and if feigned resistance is the subtlest ruse of collaboration, how, fifty-five years after the fact, could one prove anything beyond a reasonable doubt?[24]

That logical stumbling block is further complicated by the temporal factor. The war, after all, lasted long enough for one to be able to spend years collaborating, then years resisting. In 1996, Boston

22. See the testimony of Gillette Chapel, the only witness to have known Papon at the time of his alleged crimes, in Dumay 1997d: "He requisitioned the means of transportation. Instead of freight trains, he ordered passenger cars. He even—*n'est-ce pas, Maurice?*—had blankets brought in."

23. See the interpretation of Laurence Greilsamer (1997): "Wasn't the primary aim of such efforts to eliminate any demonstration of compassion on the part of the Bordeaux population toward the persecuted families?" And a letter from Papon to the German police supporting this interpretation is quoted.

24. See ibid., where Papon is cited: "By character, I had no predilection to desert; by ideology, I remained faithful to the instructions given by London to functionaries and magistrates [to remain on the job]."

University gave an honorary doctorate to Maurice Druon, a man of impeccable wartime credentials at Radio London and subsequently permanent secretary of the French Academy. A few months later he showed up as a witness *for the defense* in the Papon trial. His argument was that from his point of view the trial had been decided when a jury of thirty-five million Frenchmen had given the presidency to a man who had been decorated by Pétain, then decorated by the Resistance, and who was fully deserving of both decorations.[25] The novelist Romain Gary once came up with a Solomonic solution: when it came to many Frenchmen who had lived through the war, one had simply to cut them in two, give a medal to one half and shoot the rest.[26] All, of course, might depend on when one made the switch. Jean Dutourd wrote memorably of those whose resistance began when they contributed their household refuse to the barricades improvised during the last weeks of the war; and indeed, a barricade was probably a better idea than a garage sale in the Paris of August 1944.[27] The key point is to see how vexed the French situation could be: A new category, the Vichysto-résistant, was the Papon trial's contribution to French parlance.[28] And even de Gaulle himself was known to refer to the Bordeaux resistance as a viper's tangle.[29]

25. See Dumay 1997d. Druon claimed to be particularly pained by the fact that the principal beneficiary of Papon's "Franco-French" trial was Germany and that consequently the "sons of the victims [were] becoming the objective allies of the sons of the executioners."

26. Gary 1979, 81. For further comments on Gary and the genocide, see my essay "The Holocaust Comedies of 'Emile Ajar' " (Mehlman 1995, 154–73).

27. See Dutourd 1952.

28. See Conan 1997c. The *vichysto-résistants* are said by Conan to constitute a "vast migratory herd" making its way, rather late in the day, from one camp to the other.

29. See Conan 1998, 203. The comment on the "viper's tangle" occurred in the testimony of Hubert de Beaufort on February 24, 1998.

(Everything, of course, is coded literarily in France. *Noeud de vipères* may have been a gesture of homage to François Mauriac, the Bordeaux author of the novel of that name.)

Back to the trial or its highlights. The historian who had launched the whole Papon affair in 1981 by discovering Papon's signature on lists of deported Jews had in the interim reversed positions and showed up as a witness *for the defense*. There had been a category error in 1981, he claimed; these were not orders for future acts but records of past ones, not what the speech act theorists call performatives but constatives.[30]

A second bombshell: Serge and Arno Klarsfeld attempted to derail the trial by revealing that the presiding judge, whom they distrusted, was a distant relative of one of the deportees.[31] Presumably, he could not be impartial. He stayed. Then the Klarsfelds broke with the state prosecution by asking for no more than ten years in prison, effectively inventing the category of the small-time (or petty) criminal against humanity.[32] Finally, just before the end of the trial, Papon's wife of more than fifty years died. He returned to the courtroom to face judgment for crimes against humanity looking

---

30. See the interview with Michel Bergès (1997): "He intervened only *a posteriori*, on orders from [Prefect Maurice] Sabatier, in order to write informative reports on the raids for his superiors—and not at all to record orders." At the trial, he testified: "He did not decide; he was a relayer of information" (Dumay 1998).

31. The revelation came in late January 1998. The implication was plainly that Jean-Louis Castagnède, the presiding judge, could not deliver a fair judgment. Serge Klarsfeld had been distrustful of the judge ever since Papon had been allowed to go free on his own cognizance at the start of the trial. Alain Finkielkraut, accusing Klarsfeld of being "memory-besotted," mordantly asked whether Castagnède was being alleged to be predisposed in Papon's favor out of gratitude for the defendant's having lopped an embarrassing branch off his family tree. See Finkielkraut 1997.

32. See Conan 1998, 265.

very much a victim. It should be said that Papon was an astonishingly eloquent and alert defendant. Many were stunned by the acuity of his allusions. As one wag put it: he may have been evil, but he certainly wasn't banal.[33] He gave a final speech that began as a eulogy for his wife and ended with an astonishing evocation of the quality of the light Rembrandt had captured in a painting of the binding of Isaac, the light on the arm of Abraham just before it is stayed, "the most truthful illumination that a great painter succeeded in bequeathing to posterity." (For anyone who has read Elie Wiesel on Isaac as figure of the first survivor of a holocaust, it is a mindboggling comparison.)[34]

The verdict? A compromise. Guilty of the crime against humanity of complicity in the illegal arrest and sequestering of a number of individuals, not guilty of any complicity in murder. It was a victory for the Klarsfelds. Papon was a petty criminal against humanity. It was, some thought, as though a suppressed desire to acquit were readable in the verdict. I thought of the oddly mixed verdict of the second Dreyfus trial: guilty with extenuating circumstances. As with the case of Dreyfus, to whom Papon had had the *culot* or *chutzpah* to compare himself, this was a compromise (on issues of ultimate import) that came at the end of a century and that felt like the end of an era.[35] For better or for worse, France had held its last trial for crimes against humanity relating to the genocide. To say that it had crucial symbolic value, that Papon bore with him the guilt of the Vichy regime, was to cast him in the role of scapegoat. That he was a guilty (rather than an

---

33. Gopnik 1998, 90.

34. Wiesel 1976, 69–97.

35. On the "monstrosity" of Papon's comparison of himself to Dreyfus, see Vidal-Naquet 1998: "That a man with that past should compare himself to Captain Dreyfus is unimaginable."

innocent) scapegoat only vexed matters further.[36] The best historians of the period lamented that the trial had effected a regression in historical understanding.[37] Papon, the guilty scapegoat, knew one last moment of notoriety. At the age of eighty-nine, just before the beginning of his prison term in October 1999, Papon, comparing himself to Victor Hugo, made a dash across the Swiss border in search of sanctuary. He was identified, then captured within days, and began serving his ten-year term in La Santé Prison in Paris.

. . .

Post scriptum (2002): In the years since his sentencing, Papon has continued to be a focus of discussion in France. Finkielkraut has argued with some eloquence that the symbolic importance attached to the case had more to do with Papon's age, as the last surviving prosecutable player in the drama, than with his actual deeds. And that it was a particularly inhumane violation of justice to punish a man for his longevity.[38] On July 25, 2002, the European Court of Human Rights, in the case of *Papon v. France*, issued a Chamber Judgment ruling that the Court of Cassation's earlier refusal of Papon's right to appeal the decision against him because he had not surrendered to custody was "a particularly severe sanction" and was, in fact, illegal. The European Court "awarded the applicant 29,192.68 euros for costs and expenses and dismissed the remainder of his claim for just satisfaction."[39]

36. The category of the "guilty scapegoat" was applied to Papon by Jean Daniel (1997).
37. See Rousso 1998: "For this specialist, the Papon trial marked a 'regression' in our historical knowledge of the dark years."
38. Finkielkraut 2002, 34.
39. European Court of Human Rights, press release of 25 July 2002.

. . .

Post post scriptum (2005): On September 19, 2002, at the age of ninety-two, Maurice Papon was freed from La Santé Prison by a surprise decision of the Paris Cour d'Appel. Humanitarian reasons, relating to the convict's advanced age and serious illness, were invoked. He had served less than a third of his sentence.

6

The Gray Zone of Scientific Invention
Primo Levi and the Omissions of Memory

NANCY HARROWITZ

PRIMO LEVI, as a Holocaust survivor and writer whose testimony *Survival in Auschwitz* is critically recognized as among the most powerful, moving, and insightful works treating the subject of the Nazi genocide, is well known for his other works as well: *The Reawakening* about his long and complicated journey home after the war, a novel, short stories that fall into the genre of science fiction, philosophical essays, poetry, and a semi-autobiographical work about his life as a chemist. Levi's topics in these works include partisans during World War II, individual responsibility and bystander complicity during the Holocaust, and the ambiguity of power relations in the camps. Offering a reasoned, subtle, and sophisticated voice in dealing with painful and complex matters, Levi's reputation is that of a writer and a philosopher living in a difficult age as a Holocaust survivor, not afraid to take on even the thorniest of issues.

But Levi was a scientist as well, trained in Fascist Italy as a chemist: in fact, he worked in this field for most of his adult life before retiring to become a full-time writer. Even though his own science was not theoretical, as Levi was a chemist working in a paint factory, he maintained a strong interest in the theoretical side of science that is expressed in some of his fiction and essays. While readers and critics are certainly aware that Levi was a chemist, the influence of his scientific background and training has not been fully appreciated. What is even more striking, however, is just how complicated Levi's connection is to science in general and how he articulates these complexities.

To further complicate his identity status vis-à-vis science, Levi attributes his surviving Auschwitz in large part to his skills as a chemist, which earned him a privileged position in the camp and spared him from a second winter of hard labor. In a sense, Levi occupies a difficult dual position as both a subject of racialist science and a practitioner of science for the racialists. He became a slave laborer in Auschwitz, because of his Jewishness, and was also a Jewish scientist, both in Auschwitz and after the war. Because of this situation, Levi's complicated identity as both a scientist and a Holocaust survivor is at the core of some complex issues that emerge from his work.

A compelling aspect to Levi's having labored in the camps as a chemist for the Nazis is the particular configuration of memory about science that comes out in his works and that would appear to be directly influenced by this difficult and complex subject position. His work as a chemist in Buna is addressed in an elliptical fashion in both *Survival in Auschwitz* (1996) and in a chapter of *The Periodic Table* (1984), as he discusses in both texts the circumstances of this labor. But it is only in two later texts that the full ramification of what it meant for Levi to use his chemistry in this way becomes apparent: namely, in *The Drowned and the Saved* (1988), published a year before his death, and in an essay about the practicing of modern science, entitled "Hatching the Cobra," which came out only a few months before the end of Levi's life.

The two texts in question elucidate at least in part the question of how Levi integrated his complicated identity as a scientist and as a survivor and what he had to say about the practicing of post-Holocaust science, given his own subject position. They also indirectly address how memory is configured in Levi's opus vis-à-vis the ways in which he articulates his complicated identity. In this essay, I will look at Levi's representation of chemistry as a discipline against the background of the Holocaust. I will also look at the story of another Jewish chemist, Fritz Haber, in order to see how this episode illuminates Levi's concerns about the responsibility and the identity of the individual scientist, and the ways in which it calls into question the issue of memory. My analysis will be divided into two parts: the first will concentrate on what Levi does discuss regarding his portrayal of science, and the second will concentrate on an episode in the history of chemistry and warfare quite relevant to Levi's concerns about science and the Holocaust, upon which he does not comment.

The text in which Levi most directly presents his views on science is *The Periodic Table*, first published in 1975. This text can well be described as an autobiography of his life as a chemist, yet we also learn of his reactions to Fascist persecution of the Jews, to the early years of the war, and to his own identity as a Jew in Italy. In general, *The Periodic Table* moves from a redemptive and religious notion of science to a critique of postwar ethics. Levi begins to criticize science for being apolitical and not able to answer his questions about the war. This criticism is particularly apparent in the chapter in which Levi recounts his postwar correspondence with Muller, who was one of the German chemists employed at Auschwitz.[1]

Some of Levi's lesser-known science fiction tales and essays on

---

[1]. For a discussion of Levi's correspondence with Muller, see Harrowitz 1998, 19–39.

science demonstrate a much more profound crisis in Levi's vision of science as progress and redemption. For example, he wrote two short stories about medical experimentation, entitled "Versamina" and "Angelic Butterfly," which make clear the dangers of the temptation of knowledge for the researcher and how easy it is to abandon all humane principles in order to further scientific research.[2]

In looking at the whole of Levi's works, these stories, with their wholesale unambivalent condemnation of the ambitious researcher, are the exception rather than the rule. In general, Levi demonstrates a more cautious approach to articulating the degree to which science became a vehicle for destruction in World War II, and what that might mean about science as a discipline. His reticence speaks to his ambivalence about the vulnerability of science and to his own difficult subject position as a scientist and survivor. But this reticence does eventually break down, at least to a certain degree. A tension between his own career as a chemist and what he thinks about science does come out in a very late essay he wrote, entitled "Hatching the Cobra" (1989).

The essay, published in September 1986 approximately seven months before his death, sheds some light on his view of the moral standing of science. Levi begins his essay with a story: in the first paragraph, he cites Pliny discussing a Sicilian tyrant, Phalaris, who had a brass bull constructed by an inventor named Perillus:

> Let no one praise Perillus, crueler than the tyrant Phalaris, for whom he built a bull, promising him that a man locked inside it would bellow when a fire was lit beneath it, and who was the first to test on himself such torture as the fruit of a cruelty more just than his. To such an extent had he distorted a most noble art, destined to

---

2. English translations of these stories may be found in Levi 1990, *The Sixth Day and Other Tales*.

represent gods and men. Thus many of his workers had labored only to build an instrument of torture! Actually, his works are preserved for only one reason: so that whoever sees them will hate the hands of their creators. (1989, 172)

In the second paragraph of the essay Levi informs us as to the longevity of the story: the tale also appears in Pindar, in Ovid, and in Dante's *Inferno*, canto 27, as a prelude to the story of Guido da Montefeltro. Levi then reviews Dante's judgment of the parable of the bull and the moral standing of the inventor, its first victim.

Perillus, as the inventor of a cruel mechanism of torture, is according to Dante a fitting victim of his own invention: "ció fu dritto," and it was just. But for Levi this is too simple a judgment on what he sees as very complex issues, and he is not content to let matters rest there. He says,

> This story, whether true or false, has a curious up-to-date flavor. For the purposes of a posthumous trial of the tyrant and his craftsmen, it would be essential to establish to which of the two should be attributed the initiative and idea for the horrendous machine. If it had been invented by Perillus and proposed to Phalaris, there is no doubt that Perillus . . . deserved to be punished (but not necessarily in this way and by Phalaris, who by accepting the artifact had become the inventor's accomplice) . . . If, on the other hand, Phalaris had commissioned the work, the eye-for-an-eye punishment adopted by him seems excessive and abusive . . . By this hypothesis, Perillus does not come out of this absolved, yet we can grant him some extenuating circumstances: perhaps he had been forced, or flattered, or threatened, or blackmailed. We don't know; but his figure as an inventor suggests modern figures and events. (1989, 173)

Levi then proposes that the figure of the modern scientist is also evoked by this tale, so it is not only the overall paradigm that brings to mind contemporary situations, but the actual figure of the scientist/inventor. His analogy is the scientist whose work is commissioned by the state either for the defense of the country or to attack a neighboring country. Levi then becomes even more specific: the tale of the bull functions as an analogy to science during World War II. He cites what he calls the "portentous collection of brains . . . that gave birth to the atomic bomb in the nick of time and to nuclear energy for peacetime use." He briefly discusses what happened to these scientists after the war: Pontecorvo changed fields for ideological reasons; others repented and changed jobs. Martin Ryle goes so far as to insist that scientific research be stopped altogether. Levi's analysis of the Phalaris/Perillus relationship demonstrates the complexity of judgments regarding inventors, inventions, and the power hierarchy; in fact, the intricate way in which he argues the case resembles his discussions of the gray zone of camp survival, found in *The Drowned and the Saved*.

How does this analogy relate to the story of the bull? Phalaris represents the modern state, and the scientists are those inventors who make mass destruction possible. The specifics of their relation are important: do the scientists create weapons on the instigation of the government or do they come up with these ideas and then propose their use? And Pliny's concerns come into play here too: will we come to hate the hand of the inventor? Will science be despised because of its creations? Levi comments on the ingeniousness of the instrument: he recognizes that devising a bull in such a way as to render the screams of the victims into what sounds like the bellowing of a bull must have been very difficult, but an appreciation of the skill involved does not weaken his moral judgment.

There is, however, a piece missing in Levi's story: what about the creation and implementation of mass destruction achieved in the concentration camps? What about the relation of modern science and technology to genocide? What this essay does not address is the role of science and technology in the Holocaust. Furthermore, that parable of the brass bull used to kill its victims through fire sounds peculiarly and eerily crematory in its method. One wonders why Levi felt compelled to relegate moral problems in science during World War II only to those scientists working on the atomic bomb, and not to those who had worked on methods of mass destruction used in the camps. The complicity of science in genocide has been well established: Robert Proctor affirms that "Nazis were able to draw on the imagery and authority of science . . . Nazi racial policy emerged from within the scientific community" (Proctor 1992, 28). Not only individual scientists, but scientific institutions as well played the role of Perillus to Hitler's Phalaris: inventing and making possible the implementation of the racialist theory leading to genocide, and its specific usage as well. Levi's own discipline of chemistry was also involved: Robert J. Lifton and Eric Markusen discuss the role of the chemists involved in the testing and use of Zyklon-B, the gas used in the gas chambers, stating that chemists "had to create and maintain the conditions and mixtures within which Zyklon-B could be stored, shipped and then converted into its deadly gaseous form" (Lifton and Markusen 1992, 103).[3]

Even though in this essay Levi has made a strong case for the potential of science to produce unbridled destruction, he ends his discussion by making an impassioned argument for continuing science. He says that "we are who we are: every one of us, even farmers, even the most modest artisans, are researchers, and we always have been. From the inherent danger in every new scientific discovery, however, we can and must defend ourselves" (Levi 1989, 176). Levi concludes

---

3. Lifton and Markusen also suggest that for some chemists during the Reich, working on methods of mass extermination was important to their careers (1992, 167).

by giving us his recipe for avoiding the dangers of science. He says that every university science department must instill in its students the necessity of questioning the outcome of their practicing of the profession.

"Don't fall in love with suspect problems," Levi says. "Don't hide behind the hypocrisy of neutral science. Find out how your research will be used, if what you are hatching is a dove, a chimera, a cobra or nothing . . . We know that the world is not just black and white and that your decision can be difficult. Accept the study of a new medicine, refuse to formulate a nerve gas" (1989, 176). In this essay Levi makes clear what he thinks moral guidelines for researchers should look like, but, as we've seen, the only specific mention of chemistry is in this brief evocation of nerve gas.

A gap appears overall in Levi's recounting and presentation of chemistry: there is a major chapter in the history of chemistry to which Levi does not refer directly, here or elsewhere. This is the military use of chemistry during World War I, also referred to as the Chemical War. This most startling omission on Levi's part involves the story of Fritz Haber, a German Jewish chemist whose story raises questions pertinent to our understanding of Levi and science. There are two ways to approach this omission: the first is to imagine as a hypothesis that Levi was very likely to have known about Haber and that there is some reason for his not mentioning him or the story of chemical involvement in either war. The second approach is to look at the story of Haber and its consequences and ramifications as illuminating in themselves for an understanding of Levi as another Jewish chemist and an understanding of Levi's own relation to the politics of science.

Fritz Haber made his scientific reputation in the years before World War I when he developed a system of nitrogen fixation making possible the manufacture of artificial fertilizer, extremely useful to developing countries. But Haber was also an ardent German nationalist: when Germany entered World War I, he began to work on systems of chemical warfare in order to shorten the war and assure victory for Germany. He was, in fact, the first chemist to develop chlorine gas to be used in World War I. Haber was anything but the academic chemist who remains in his laboratory. After developing a system of delivering the poison gas, he oversaw its field operations, directing the military as to the best possible conditions in which to use the gas, which was first employed against the French on April 22, 1915, with Haber present in the field. Haber became the head of a newly formed chemical warfare department for the German government and held military titles until the end of the war. His principal complaint about the military during that period was that they did not understand the potential of his new weapon and thus did not take full advantage of it, and that this is why Germany lost the war.

Deeply unsettled after Germany's defeat, Haber was a hero in his own country but vilified elsewhere, especially in France and in England, both by the general public and by leading scientists in those countries because of his advocacy of poison gas. Nonetheless, in 1920 Haber won a Nobel prize in chemistry for 1918 for his nitrogen fixation principles, a Nobel contested because of his wartime work. But the memory of the people and of science too was short regarding Haber's ostracism: he quickly became one of the most famous scientists in the world, both for his invention of nitrogen fixation principles, which allowed underdeveloped countries to develop fertilizer for agriculture, and because he was also "one of the earliest and most successful scientists to forge a tie between research and industry" (Stern 1999, 61). The figure of Haber swings wildly between his humanitarian contributions, which were considerable, and his equally intense involvement in the destruction of people through gas warfare.

The Kaiser Wilhelm Institute for Chemistry was established and Haber remained its director until 1933. Haber had converted to Protestantism as a career move in 1892 after years of professional delays because of his Jewishness.[4] Yet, despite his ambivalence about Judaism, Haber strongly identified with other Jews: "most of his friends were Jews or of Jewish descent" (Stern 1999, 74). When the Nazis took power in 1933, Jewish academics lost their jobs soon thereafter, after the Enabling Act went into force and the Nazis drafted a new law removing non-Aryan professors from their jobs. As director of the institute, Haber could have stayed, but he resigned out of outrage at the firing of so many of his Jewish colleagues.

Haber was then welcomed in England by scientific colleagues. We could read this welcome as owing largely to his change of status: no longer a state- and military-backed perpetrator of poison gas, Haber was now a victim of Nazi discrimination, and scientific ranks closed around him. He was invited to Palestine to visit Chaim Weitzmann, who considered him to be one of the world's greatest scientists. Haber accepted, but died in England in January 1934 before he could go.

The liminal and problematic status of Haber's Jewish identity deserves a chapter in itself. Both of his wives were Jewish, as were most of his friends and colleagues. His family constitutes a complicated genealogical frame in which to ponder the issues that his story raises. One of the most tragic episodes is the fate of his first wife, Clara, also a Jewish chemist, who had developed her own very promising career before marrying Haber. She became an unhappy housewife and mother when she gave up her career to stay at home with their

---

4. For a compelling discussion of the ambivalences surrounding the issue of conversion faced by not only Fritz Haber but many other German Jews of his generation, see Stern 1999, 74–76.

child. As a chemist, however, she fully understood the ramifications of Haber's development of poison gas and the horrors of this weapon. She pleaded with her husband not to develop it, but Haber's strong German nationalism prevailed. A couple of weeks after he employed poison gas against the French, Clara committed suicide, leaving no explanation behind.

Clara's protest against poison gas and her husband's involvement came in the form of tragically silencing her own voice. Other family members, however, have spoken about the Haber story, each in their own way. His second wife, Charlotta, has written a book about her life with Haber, and their son, Ludwig, also a chemist, published a history of chemical warfare in 1986 entitled *The Poisonous Cloud* (1986). There are other commentators as well: Tony Harrison has written a play centering on the Haber story, *Square Rounds* (1992). The Harrison play points out the greatest tragic irony of the Haber story: the weapon that Haber in his nationalistic zeal developed for use against the Allies in World War I was ultimately used, albeit in a different form, to kill millions of Jews in World War II. But even Harrison, very harsh in his judgment of Haber, does not have the story quite right: the connections are even closer than this. After World War I, Haber worked on gases to be used against agricultural pests. As Fritz Stern comments, "Haber and his institute experimented with pesticides and developed a deadly substance that came to be known as Zyklon-B. The horror of Haber's involvement with the gas that later murdered millions, including friends and distant relatives, beggars description" (Stern 1999, 135).

How does the complicated and tragic story of Fritz Haber fit into Levi's concept of the interrelations among science, society, and the memory of the Holocaust that permeates Levi's thinking? Let us first look at the omission of this history: Haber was so well known as an internationally acclaimed—and defamed—figure, and his contribution to gas warfare so widely discussed, that we can take as a working hypothesis that Levi must have known about Haber. In the light of the ambivalent story of Fritz Haber, Levi's very lack of acknowledgment of this most problematic chapter in the history of chemistry and in the history of Jewish scientists is remarkable, especially given that he dedicates the essay I've discussed, "Hatching the Cobra," to the topic of responsible use of science. In that essay Levi cites the development of the atom bomb as his example of wartime collaboration between scientists and the government. It would seem that the Haber story would have been equally compelling in terms of the problematic nature of the relationship of science to war. Certainly the role of German chemists in the administration of Zyklon-B at the death camps could have illustrated Levi's concerns about war and science, but here perhaps we are a bit too close to home for Levi. The only indication of this lacuna is that nervous mention of nerve gas as a research subject to avoid—yet Levi does not pursue this topic, concentrating instead on the atomic bomb as his example.

A brief look at two texts in which Levi portrays his chemist mentor Ludwig Gattermann can further inform us as to the nature of his silence on gas warfare and on the complicity of chemistry in the Holocaust. In his book *A Search for Roots*, Levi examines authors who have been especially important to his own formation as a thinker and writer. One of these figures is the German chemist Ludwig Gattermann (1860–1920), the author of *A Practical Handbook for Organic Chemists*. This was an essential text to the practice of chemistry, one that Levi first read when he was twenty-two years old and that became a constant companion throughout his career. Levi introduces his favorite pages from Gattermann's text in the following manner, calling the Gatterman excerpt "The Words of the Father":

> To include among my favorite readings these three pages from my old copy of *Practical Organic Chemistry* is not meant to be a provocation. In thirty years of profession I have consulted them hundreds of times, I have almost memorized them, I've never found an error in them, and they have perhaps silently turned aside troubles for me, my colleagues and the tasks entrusted to me. (Levi 1981, 83; translation mine)

The three pages that Levi reproduces are entitled "For the prevention of accidents" and contain not only strict admonitions about the danger of certain chemicals used in conjunction with others, but practical remedies for injuries caused by particular situations and what to keep on hand for first aid. One cannot help but think of a metaphorical weight in those elliptical words Levi uses in his introduction regarding these pages of Gattermann's having "perhaps silently turned aside troubles for me." Levi's knowledge and subsequent use of Gattermann in Auschwitz do in fact suggest the warding off of an accident, as by his own accounts the position as a chemist that Gattermann permitted him to attain allowed him small privileges and an easier second winter in the camp than he otherwise would have had. The listing of remedies for accidents as well as their prevention in Gattermann's text, together with Levi's embrace of Gattermann as a father whose wise words could help to prevent or remedy accidents, also foster a view of the war as a kind of disastrous chemical outcome—first aid required to repair the damage done, and a manual like Gattermann's as an essential tool. It implies, moreover, that damages *can* be repaired. This implication runs directly contrary to Levi's thoughts on the condition of survivors, permanently damaged by their treatment; as he comments, "once again it must be observed, mournfully, that the injury cannot be healed: it extends through time" (*The Drowned and the Saved*, 24). Levi's portrayal of Gattermann reinforces the general sense that Levi often projects in his writings about science, that science ultimately should provide an escape from situations whose remedies are elusive.

In Levi's testimony *Survival in Auschwitz*, he refers directly to Gattermann in the chapter entitled "Chemical Examination," when Levi is tested to see if his background in chemistry could be useful in the production of artificial rubber at the camp. But here Gattermann appears in a more ambivalent light. Before going to this chemical examination, Levi asks himself the following question, which I would argue is fully comprehensible only against the backdrop of the Haber story: "But have the Germans such a great need for chemists?" (Levi 1996, 103).

This episode is central to Levi's survival in the camp, and he frames his narration of the exam through an explanation of what was required even to present oneself at such an event, after living as a slave laborer in the conditions of Auschwitz. The prisoners who have decided to take the exam discuss how they will manage to overcome this clash in identity. One of their number, Clausner, shows Levi the bottom of his soup bowl, upon which he has written, "ne pas chercher à comprendre" (don't try to understand).

Levi reads this note in the more general terms of the status of thought in the camp: "Although we do not think for more than a few minutes a day, and then in a strangely detached and external manner, we well know that we will end in selections . . . And now I also know that I can save myself if I become a Specialist, and that I will become a Specialist if I pass a chemistry examination" (1996, 103).

Levi manages to close the gaping chasm between what he has become in the camp and his former intellectual self, but not without some difficulty. His analysis of the German chemist administering the oral examination, the matters debated, and the fact that his discipline could have been seriously discussed in such a place and in such a way is revealing. This is how he describes his encounter with this colleague in chemistry:

> When he finished writing, he raised his eyes and looked at me. From that day on, I have thought about Dr. Pannwitz many times and in many ways. I have asked myself how he really functioned as a man; how he filled his time, outside of the polymerization and the Indo-Germanic consciousness; above all when I was once more a free man, I wanted to meet him again, not from a spirit of revenge, but merely from a personal curiosity about the human soul.
>
> Because that look was not one between two men; and if I had known how completely to explain the nature of that look, which came as if across the glass window of an aquarium between two human beings who live in different worlds, I would also have explained the essence of the great insanity of the third Germany. (Levi 1996, 105–6)

Because Pannwitz is a colleague, because he and Levi share this fundamental professional activity of chemistry, his bigotry toward Levi is that much more intolerable. Nevertheless, chemistry does eventually serve as an ambivalent link between them. Pannwitz treats Levi as if he were subhuman until Levi begins to recount the details of his work in chemistry at the university. The language of racism cedes at least in part to the language of science, and Pannwitz quite literally uses Gattermann's book as a common bond between the two chemists. Levi's reaction to Gattermann is one of familiarity and discomfort at the same time: "[H]e shows me Gattermann's book, and even this is absurd and impossible, that down here, on the other side of the barbed wire, a Gattermann should exist, exactly similar to the one I studied in Italy in my fourth year, at home" (Levi 1996, 105).

Gattermann is Levi's salvation, as this text provides a professional link between him and Pannwitz and also represents the knowledge of chemistry that saves him, but it is a strangely ambivalent portrayal as well. Gattermann was after all a German chemist, representing a more benevolent German culture before the Third Reich. Levi resists any connection between that Germany and this one, on the other side of the barbed wire, as he puts it. The Gattermann he studied was at home in Italy, part of the international language and community of science, not a localized Gattermann, used in the death camps to exploit slave labor in the German war effort.

These two conflicting portrayals of Gattermann—one presented nostalgically but elliptically in *A Search for Roots* and the other a Gattermann tainted by his usefulness on "the other side of the barbed wire"—put forward Levi's ambivalence about the potential uses of his chosen field. In these two portrayals, these uses range from Gattermann's benevolent and paternal efforts to save his colleagues in chemistry from disastrous accidents or, when accidents cannot be prevented, to aid in their succor, to an exploitation of chemical training for the direct benefit of the Nazi war effort through the attempted manufacture of artificial rubber. The distance between these possibilities represents the first part of the story of Levi's omission of chemistry's more serious complicity in the Third Reich.

As I've noted, the great unwritten chapter in Levi's representation of his discipline is the story of Haber, chemistry, and World War I. What makes this omission even more problematic is its genealogical relation to Levi's own situation and to the Holocaust. Given that Levi was incarcerated in the camps and that the ultimate legacy of Haber's poison gas was in fact Zyklon-B, Levi's brief mention of nerve gas as a formulation to avoid speaks volumes through his subsequent silence. His terse mention is a lead that he refuses to follow, despite its intense personal and genealogical weight.

In *The Periodic Table*, Levi uses the terms *militant chemist* and *militant chemistry* several times, as a way of attempting to bridge that gap he has identified between the social/political context and the world of ideas to which he is so strongly attracted. The category of militancy that Levi refers to informs us as to the potentially political nature of Levi's chemistry. *Militant*, like *military*, comes from *milus*, meaning "soldier," but in English, *militant* is stronger and more aggressive than in Italian, where there are two primary uses of the term. In Italian it can indicate an active member of one's profession or group, like "the militant church," meaning an involved, active church. Levi's use of the term, however, is most likely modeled after its meaning in the phrase *la critica militante*, or "militant criticism," a term that became popular in Italy during the late sixties and seventies and that indicates involvement in the politics of the time—in other words, "engagement." In the Haber episode, we have what was really an active, militant chemistry . . . but on the wrong side of the fence for Levi; in other words, a militancy in the English sense that puts chemistry and chemists in the driver's seat of aggressive nationalistic warfare, a position absolutely antithetical to what Levi desires from science and to what he thinks science should do. What resonance does Levi's understanding of militant chemistry have against the background of the Haber story?

For Levi, it is easier to occlude the memory of this truly militant chemistry almost entirely, to pretend that chemistry has gone from alchemy—suspect, perhaps, but not, after all, homicidal—to benign chemical theories inappropriately disengaged from the war around them. Levi's shunning of scientific memory is motivated by a deep love and nostalgia for his own profession, which sets limits on the kind of critique and representation of chemistry he is able to perform. And it is motivated by another phenomenon as well: a liminal status and ensuing anxiety regarding his own identity as a Jewish chemist, an identity heavily mediated by his Holocaust experience and by his experience as a literary writer.

Levi's identities as a Jew and as a chemist became intertwined to a certain degree during his university years because of the anti-Semitic Racial Laws in Italy, but a complicated and problematic merger of these two identities becomes patently manifest during his stay at Auschwitz. Because of his Jewishness, he was deported and became a slave laborer there. But he attributes his survival of Auschwitz in large part to his skills as a chemist, which earned him a privileged position in the camp and spared him from a second winter of hard labor. However, this privileged position in turn raises the question of participation: while Levi clearly was not a willing and enthusiastic collaborator like Haber, nonetheless, according to his own statements, his work as a chemist for the Germans put him into a "gray zone" vis-à-vis his scientific identity and its relation to his Jewishness. Needless to say, this is not how Levi was or ever would be judged by the world: it can be read rather as a manifestation of his own shame and guilt, emotions that he articulates eloquently—albeit in a largely impersonal way—in *The Drowned and the Saved*. In his essays therein entitled "The Gray Zone" and "Shame," Levi discusses his survival and that of other privileged camp inmates. In a controversial passage to which other survivors have taken exception, Levi maintains that the truly good all perished and suggests that the survivors were not on the same moral plane as those who died.

It is crucial to read this polemical statement in the context in which Levi presents it in his essay. Levi explains that a friend of his visited him after his return and suggested to him that his survival was not chance:

> He told me that my having survived could not be the work of chance, of an accumulation of fortunate circumstances (as I did then and still do maintain) but rather of Providence. I bore the mark, I was an elect: I, the nonbeliever, and even less of a believer

after the season of Auschwitz, was a person touched by Grace, a saved man. And why me? It is impossible to know, he answered. Perhaps because I had to write and by writing bear witness: wasn't I in fact then, in 1946, writing a book about my imprisonment? (Levi 1988, 82)

Levi rejects this argument to the point of casting aspersions on other survivors:

> The "saved" of the Lager were not the best, those predestined to do good, the bearers of a message: what I had seen and lived through proved the exact contrary. Preferably the worst survived, the selfish, the violent, the insensitive, the collaborators of the "gray zone," the spies. It was not a certain rule (there were none, nor are there certain rules in human matters), but it was nevertheless a rule. I felt innocent, yes, but enrolled among the saved and therefore in permanent search of a justification in my own eyes and those of others. The worst survived, that is, the fittest; the best all died. (Levi 1988, 82)

This extreme statement, while disturbing and unfair to survivors, illuminates Levi's unsettled self-deprecation regarding his survival more than it elucidates the question of why some survived the camps. I would also maintain that it points directly to an underlying issue of collaboration and to the burden that the thought of collaboration imposed on Levi. His first statement above helps to contextualize his argument, as we see that the notion of his surviving for some higher reason is very offensive to him. But does he truly believe that it was only "an accumulation of fortunate circumstances" that allowed him to survive? Was it only fortunate that he was a chemist who spoke enough German to survive linguistically in the camp? Does he view his use of his chemical skills at the artificial rubber plant in Buna as survival or as a necessary collaboration, and how does one tell them apart under these circumstances? Part of his essay entitled "The Gray Zone" is in fact based on a subtle and intelligent understanding of how difficult it is to judge on a moral plane low-level participation in the hierarchy of the camp. Levi makes very clear distinctions between victims and perpetrators in his argument, discussing the taking advantage of small privileges, and so forth, as long as they do not hurt others, although he also discusses the necessity of thievery even from fellow prisoners. But is this kind of small participation, which he judges as essentially blameless, on the same level as participating in the Nazis' effort to produce artificial rubber, which could have immensely furthered their war effort and have been used against the Allies? Once again, it is not my place to judge Levi for his taking the position in the camp as a chemist—if anything, his readers are grateful to him for taking the opportunity to survive; they are not judgmental and certainly not inclined to see this means of survival as collaboration. It is Levi's own attitude toward his own work and how this work might have influenced his feelings toward chemistry that is revealing here. In the strongly articulated and bitter essays that form *The Drowned and the Saved*, three poles of reference guide his arguments: issues of memory (it is no accident that the first chapter is entitled "The Memory of the Offense" and challenges the reliability of memory and its manipulation factor especially for perpetrators), guilt, and collaboration. These three also inform his views toward science.

The questions that must be asked are these: Is Levi's articulation of the history of science indebted to his own memory of what it meant to be working for the Nazis as a chemist in Buna? What did this work mean in light of Levi's subsequent career? How did it influence his understanding of the history and even the culture of chemistry within which he trained?

The memory of a Jewish chemist perpetrator, like Haber, evokes not a subtle self-blaming taint of collaboration under the choice of life or death, but rather the issue of direct collaboration, and perhaps this is another reason for Levi's profound silence on the subject of Haber and gas warfare. Levi's strategy of omission is his way of remembering this chapter of the history of chemistry. Another way to think about this scientific memory is to think of it in terms of a genealogical frame for the relationship between Haber and Levi. Looking at it this way helps us to understand what it meant for Levi to be part of the next generation of chemists after Haber. Levi in a sense has paid the price for the marriage of nationalism, industry, and science that Haber espoused. Levi's interest in the way we remember the history of science reflects what is at stake for him as a post-Holocaust Jewish chemist.

Memory and the Victim

7

Elie Wiesel and the Morality of Fiction

GEOFFREY HARTMAN

> "Doesn't the Talmud say that after the coming of the Messiah, the dead will rise from their graves and crawl all the way to the Holy Land?"
>
> "Not our dead, Pedro. Our dead have no graves."
>
> Pedro turned to stare out the window.
>
> "We are their graves," he replied after a long silence.
>
> Elie Wiesel, *Twilight*

THE EULOGIES ON THE OCCASION of Elie Wiesel's Nobel Peace Prize announce an ethical and inspirational ideal. It seems clear and uncomplicated. "From the abyss of the death camps," we read, Elie Wiesel "has come as a messenger to mankind—not with a message of hate and revenge but with one of brotherhood and atonement. Elie Wiesel is not only the man who survived, he is also the spirit which has triumphed" (Wiesel 1986). But in his acceptance speech the honoree refuses to shift the emphasis entirely to the living, or to a triumphant message that elides the continuing cycle of revenge and hate. It is not conventional modesty alone that makes him reply, "No one may speak for the dead, no one may interpret their mutilated dreams and visions."

Yet speak for the dead is precisely what he does—*in fiction*. Dreams and visions: this is where poet and novelist enter, and where, through them, the multitudes who perished continue to make their claim. Jews were to be despoiled not only of their life but also of their spiritual influence. No one would remember their dream of righteousness, their fidelity to a law that underwrote an intricate mixture of mercy and legal rigor. All of Elie Wiesel's writings fulfill a pledge: "I will defeat our murderers by attempting to reconstruct what they destroyed."

Wiesel refers in his speech to those who died in the Holocaust. "I sense their presence. I always do. . . . The presence of my parents, that of my little sister. The presence of my teachers, my friends, my companions." The full weight of those words is felt only after reading his novels. They portray survivors and their children who cannot forget the dead. The past within them is always about to dissolve the present. Their interior monologue is often so intense, so self-haunting, that they no longer know where they are, as the milieu shifts confusingly. Are they in Brooklyn, or in Galicia, or searching for a mass murderer in a German town after the war?

Wiesel's protagonists are burdened by thoughts that include revenge as well as feelings of unworthiness that they should be alive, or alive in the place of another. But they seek to turn a disabling into a creative melancholy. They hold to a moral order, a teaching more than two millennia old. To quote Psalm 19, it makes the simple wise, rejoices the heart, and produces a "clean fear of the Lord" (*jirat adonai tehorah*, verse 16). Yet what if this fear—this awe—is now unclean?

For the *tremendum* of the Shoah has not only implanted hate for the perpetrators but also bitterness toward God. The fear of the Lord takes its origin today not only from precepts of a just moral order, or from a sense of impurity as we approach the precincts of holiness, but also from the impossibility of theodicy. "The devil himself," Hayyim Nahman Bialik once said, "is incapable of imagining a vengeance that would redeem the blood of an infant." If mankind is made in the image of God, what kind of God does His creation reflect? *The Forgotten* expresses in the bond between father and son an enigma with theological overtones. The son is placed in the position of having to undo a curse, or dispel a secret. In Freud's concept of family romance, it is the mother whom the son wants to rescue; here it is the father who has to be redeemed. (The younger women, in these novels, are generally self-willed, sensuous presences, intent on seducing the brooding survivor back into life.) The very word "Father," in *The Forgotten*, conveys a fundamental relation, like Martin Buber's "I-Thou"; to be exact, that word turns into a despairing vocative seeking to establish a relationship once more, one that would save the Father from an encroaching amnesia more devastating than the traumatic return of memories. It is an amnesia that makes the reader fear for God as a Father, as if God Himself were losing his mind and forgetting creation. Can God get Alzheimer's?

Who is being addressed, when we read the following in *Twilight*:

> Father, I saw everything, I heard everything as I lay there among the corpses. The corpses protected me, Father. I waited until nightfall to climb out of the pit. I ran away from the dead, from their staring eyes, their tangled bodies. I ran like a wild animal until I found a stream where I washed the blood from my face, my hands, my clothes. I looked like a slaughterer. I moved only at night. I saw the mass graves, the ones in Stanislav and in Kamenetz-Podolsk. I understood that the same fate was awaiting all Jews, make no mistake. I had to tell you this, Father. Now that you know, what will you do? What will we do? (Wiesel 1987, 111)

The mythical descent of the living to the realm of the dead is a daily reality in the memory of survivors. In a series of brilliant inventions,

Wiesel shows they cannot forget; they can only go mad, or become a living Yizker book, reenacting legendary characters in a sad *commedia del arte*. Or, as in *The Fifth Son* (Wiesel 1985b), they confuse the dead and the living: the child taken away usurps the child that struggles for its own, independent life. We who were born afterward say easily enough, let there be new life, and even they say, let there be new life, but the dead still inhabit both generations too intimately.

How, then, will a novelist, who is their messenger, separate the living from the dead; how will he disentangle the survivors, or their children, or young people in general, from "mutilated dreams and visions"?

• • •

In *Dawn* (Wiesel 1982a), whose frame is the fight against the British in Palestine, the terrorist's quest is to get beyond fear, clean or unclean. But Elisha's memory, in the long wait for the dawn when he must execute a British hostage, retraces his journey from victim to terrorist in terms of a dialogue with the dead. The simple plot dissolves into a chorus of phantoms. There is always a moment when the narrator enters a conscious dream, a dream that recapitulates the lost vision of those who have died. Then "Time does not matter, only the tale does" (Wiesel 1985b, 201).

Memory should become, Wiesel has said, an "irresistible power," one that gives the dead their due, that tells their story—rather, brings them back to tell their story, even if it was buried with them in an unknown place. Only then is there a chance for catharsis, and so, perhaps, a "clean fear." But his writings show how difficult that purification is.

In *Twilight*, Raphael, whose name signifies healing, commits himself to a clinic, in the manner of a would-be psychiatrist to a training analysis. Many characters in these novels try on madness and so run the risk of becoming mad. Raphael needs this halfway house in which the inmates identify with biblical characters. The novelist shuttles by montage between the destroyed communities and the living dead of the clinic. A strange fire, a different holocaust, claimed Nadav and his brother Avihu. "I am nothing but a handful of ashes. My face is made of ashes. My chest is filled with ashes. And yet, the fire has never gone out" (Wiesel 1987, 114–17). A moment before listening to Nadav, Raphael was in his father's house, as Aharon Lipkin plans to escape from a Galicia under German rule. Now, through Nadav, he is reminded of another father, the biblical Aaron, who disappears into sadness—the sadness of a leader isolated by the need to make decisions.

Characters like Nadav are mainly voices, memory transfusions from the Bible. "If there were such a thing as song personified," Raphael says, "it would be Nadav." Can the reader accept such poetry, the irruption of ecstasy into extreme suffering?

" 'Don't touch me,' says Nadav. 'One must never touch the dead.' " That is a priest's horror of impurity returning. The one not to be touched is, ironically, the person trying to live normally. Nadav and Avihu, the children of Aaron, offered "strange fire" and were consumed. Is not our effort to justify God after the Holocaust (an effort disguised as theories attempting to justify fiction after—or about—the Holocaust) also a strange fire? We simulate a phoenix in the ashes. When love and joy return, they prove unstable; even in a freed Jerusalem the restored dream falters. "The sky is not filled with stars but with funeral candles . . . the eyes of death, the eyes of the dead stolen by death from the living" (Wiesel 1985b, 145).[1]

---

1. Even more haunting is Wiesel's portrait of Zelig, the sky-gazer, in *Twilight*, 172–73. "Like Zelig, Raphael sees a trail of glittering stars set like gravestones in a velvet sky. He sees dead men and women entranced by a mute speaker."

• • •

Part of me, I admit, resists such pathos. It prefers the broken speech of survivor testimony: "Je n'ai pas eu peur. J'ai déshabillé des morts. J'ai vu tous les jours des morts, la mort c'était pour moi comme fumer une cigarette" (I felt no fear. I stripped the dead. I saw corpses every day, death for me was like smoking a cigarette) (Wiesel 1995b). Or the concise style of Wiesel's *One Generation After* (1970): "The victims elect to become witnesses." Yet another part of me is drawn in; who else, with the exception of Agnon as inspiring and daunting precursor, incorporates so much Haggadah in his fiction? Wiesel, without removing the focus from the fate of the Jews, finds within his tradition, from Bible and midrash to Nahman of Bratslav and modern Yiddish storytellers, figures and scenes that bring the tragedy home to everyone. Through the process of novelistic discovery, this teller of tales—and he is preeminently that—prepares us for the future. It is not a triumphant future but rather, quite simply, one that gives a voice to all victims, from Kolyma as well as Auschwitz, non-Jewish as well as Jewish, honoring the many mutilated visions that afflict us because of an unabated, even unabashed, racism.

• • •

Fiction is a mode of silence, under the constraint of eloquence. Words overcome a sense of their guilt and are wounded by that success. An imaginary dialogue in *One Generation After* is explicit on that score. " '*What are you doing now?*' 'I am a sculptor. And you?' 'I write.' '*The way you say that* . . .' 'What do you expect? Millions of human beings had to die so that you might become a sculptor and I, a story-teller' " (Wiesel 1970, 8). A voice out of the whirlwind, which is our own voice, commands us to be silent, to lay Job's finger on our lips. How do we learn to stutter again?

I need not add that the Matter of the Holocaust, more than other matters of epic devastation, holds an entire civilization, the words and images that constitute it, accountable. After the hate-speech we have known, and that continues to incite murder and genocide, what good words are possible? You may call such reflections morbid, but I do not say we should succumb to them, only that they shadow us even in our best moments, our most creative moments.

There are those, like Karl Kraus or Shakespeare's Thersites or the Juvenilian satirist, whose indignant rage is so strong that no euphemism survives. But they tend to generate, therefore, more hate-speech, rather than a purgative and renovating awe. Mixed with carnivalesque laughter or biting wit, as in Brecht or Beckett, savage speech sometimes does release us. "Damn relaxes," as Blake said. But the other part of his proverb runs, "Blessing braces."

Wiesel, despite the impossibility of theodicy, or of euphemism concerning both human actions and God's inaction, husbands a tradition that preserves the good name. The dead cannot praise, the Holocaust dead cannot even be laid to rest. The morality of his fiction as fiction is to achieve a *gilgul* of the uprooted, traumatized, and dispossessed, as in *A Beggar in Jerusalem* (1985a). Working against the grain of modern realism, he even attempts a sympathetic portrayal of the *Judenrat*. Yet blessing the memory of the dead or the conscience of the survivors has its bitter antithesis in accusation: in a satanic or righteous malevolence, shown by Sam in *The Trial of God* (1979a) or by the anonymous accuser of Pedro in *Twilight*.

· · ·

No one reads Wiesel without admiring his versatile storytelling in all the genres: novel, drama, parable, essay, midrashic or hasidic exemplum, novella, autobiography. Yet the specter of the impotence of words, even of the divine word, is always present. I want to illustrate this presence, in conclusion, by two episodes that have no direct link to the Shoah, though today they cannot be read outside of that context.

The first is a personal reminiscence about the young Elie, who asks his rebbe not to attend his bar mitzvah. The reason: "To speak with you present would be like playing teacher in front of my teacher." His rebbe refuses the request. He is not expecting the boy to be a master, only to prepare to accomplish "his duty as messenger and witness." "To the astonishment of my parents and friends," the story concludes, "I went through the ceremony without a speech."[2]

What does that speechlessness indicate? A failure of nerve, an adolescent's exaggerated desire for perfection? The anecdote leaves something unsaid. Immediately before it another story is told, about a disciple who approaches a Hasidic Master with the confession that he has lost his faith in man and God. What should he do? When the reply comes, not unexpectedly, "Go and study," the disciple admits he opens the Talmud and stays on the same page months on end. He is paralyzed. Instead of an answer, Pinhas of Koretz tells the disciple about his own episode of paralyzing doubt. "I tried study, prayer, meditation. In vain. Fasting, penitence, silence. In vain. My doubts remained doubts, my questions remained open. Then, one day, I learned that Rebbe Israel Baal Shem-Tov would be coming to our town. Curiosity led me to the house where he was praying. When I entered he was finishing the *Amidah*. He turned around and the intensity in his eyes overwhelmed me. I knew he was not looking at me alone, yet I knew that I was less alone. Suddenly, without a word, I

---

2. This and the following stories are found in Wiesel's *One Generation After* (1970, 87–90). The second story is also found, with slight variations, in Wiesel's *Four Hasidic Masters* (1978).

was able to go home, open the Talmud and plunge into my studies once more."

"Without a word" reinforces the wordless intensity of the look of the Besht when he finishes the *Amidah* and turns around. The *Amidah* has a prelude: "O Lord, open Thou my lips, and my mouth shall declare Thy praise." This is, in a way, the signature tune of the Master of the Good Name. It asks God for two things: to enable us to speak, and to speak blessings—words of praise and acknowledgment, but also words characterized by a clean fear. I glimpse here less a *ba'al kol* than a *bat kol*, an echo of God's voice that resounds even in silence. The *bat kol* is all that remains when open vision and prophecy depart from Israel; it is usually portrayed as a heavenly voice, but also as something the anguished soul experiences accidentally—for example, by opening the Bible and stumbling on a passage that has the effect of a cautionary voice, even an oracle. The accident is invested with providential force.

• • •

In Wiesel, the Classical Jewish heritage has become such a *bat kol*; we respond to Elie Wiesel, to his parables and fictions, because we continue to sense a precariousness within his eloquence. In part this precariousness comes from a mystical streak that knows the debility of words and wishes to change them into something more embodied, like the wonderful gaze of the Baal Shem-Tov. According to the mystics, as we approach the Divine Countenance, "the world is transformed into a face, a thousand faces. Words turn into faces, as does light, as does fear, as does prayer" (Wiesel 1987, 115–16). The poet-novelist too seeks this transformation.

But the hazard of Wiesel's writing comes also from another source. He has said that survival during the Holocaust was accidental, for the divine word was stifled during that time (Wiesel 1998, 103). It is as if his fiction turned to Bible, Talmud, and Jewish lore out of a concern that their muteness might continue. There is mystery in the fact that they have not fallen silent before, that Jews continue to identify with a spiritual heritage tied to so much pain and horror. Would it not be better, as *The Oath*'s sad and witty plot suggests (1973), to cut the link between Jewish memory and Jewish suffering by giving up the role of memory, of transgenerational witness?

Yet even that desire for silence demands to be recognized and transmitted. The teller of tales is haunted by ghostly characters that want to rest yet cannot do so until his pages provide a requiem (Wiesel 1970, 253). In Agnon, tale and diction fuse: a vanishing Yiddish world is evoked without false vitalism by the intricate vitality of the author's Hebrew, which Emmanuel Levinas has called a "resuscitated language, beginning again with its own trace" (Levinas 1996, 130). Wiesel, steeped in the same world, which has now receded still further, and writing (after the first version of his first novel) neither in Yiddish nor Hebrew, struggles against silence to achieve a compensatory eloquence in a diasporic language.

• • •

At the end of *A Beggar in Jerusalem*, the narrator feels unable to insert a wish, as custom demands, into the *kotel* liberated by the six-day war. He hesitates to sign the paper in the name of his parents; and the novel's dream-*gilgul*, its wish-fulfilling reconstruction of orthodoxy, breaks down. Recovering, however, he then affirms the dream in their place, affirms the Name through the names of the dead. Are not Elie Wiesel's writings always a wish placed in the wall of a ruined Temple? They keep the hope alive that fiction will delay, rather than hasten, the demise of the *bat kol*.

8

Transfusing Memory
Second-Generation Postmemory in Elie Wiesel's *The Forgotten*

ALAN L. BERGER

> If there is a single theme that dominates all my writings, all my obsessions, it is that of memory—because I fear forgetfulness as much as hatred and death.
>
> Elie Wiesel, *From the Kingdom of Memory*

THE FORGOTTEN, Elie Wiesel's powerful meditation on post-Auschwitz Jewish memory (1992), intensely focuses the key question of who will bear witness for the witnesses. Elhanan Rosenbaum, a widower, is a survivor and psychotherapist suffering from Alzheimer's disease. His memory progressively deteriorating, Elhanan ["merciful God"] seeks to transmit his memory to his son Malkiel ["God is my king"], the second generation, and to remind God ["the source of all memory"] of Auschwitz. The novel in fact is an eloquent, extended, and intricate parable dealing with both the fate of Holocaust memory when survivors no longer live among us, and the complex relationship between God and memory of the Shoah. Asking what happens when a *survivor forgets*, Wiesel emphasizes the role increasingly played by the second generation in bearing witness to the Holocaust.

This essay explores Wiesel's understanding of post-Holocaust memory transmission by employing the concept of "postmemory." Marianne Hirsch defines postmemories as "the deferred effects of the traumatic experiences of both individual parents and entire communities—often transmitted in the form of seemingly strange behavior and fragmentary narratives—upon subsequent generations, which can never fully understand or appropriate these memories as their own" (Geller 2002, 250). Focusing on Wiesel's question *can memory, like blood, be transfused? The Forgotten* reveals both the synergy and the dissonance between survivors and the second generation. I explore this phenomenon by analyzing the father-son relationship, rituals of acquiring Holocaust postmemory, and Wiesel's fundamental query: what of God in all of this. I first begin, however, by briefly reflecting on the author's understanding of the dilemma of memory. I then summarize Wiesel's depiction of postmemory in his three earlier second-generation novels. I conclude by offering a meditation on *The Forgotten* as Wiesel's prayer that both God and the second generation embrace Holocaust memory.

The Dilemma of Memory

Memory is the linchpin of Wiesel's vast oeuvre. He constantly demands that both God and humanity remember the fate of the Jewish people in Europe. But memory implies more than mentally recovering something that occurred in the past, or something that has been forgotten. The claims of memory impel one to action, as in the assertion of the rabbis of antiquity, *zachor v'shamor b' dibar echad* (remembering and observing are the same thing). In Wiesel's case, "observing" means bearing witness to the Holocaust. Probing the meaning of what it means to remember, the Nobel Peace laureate writes, "It is to live in more than one world, to prevent the past from fading and to call upon the future to illuminate it. It is to revive fragments of existence, to rescue lost beings, to cast harsh light on faces and events, to drive back the sands that cover the surface of things, to combat oblivion and to reject Death" (Wiesel 1995a, 150). This admonition carries with it the survivor's moral authority. But to what do the survivors' children bear witness?

Memory requires one to act in a way that seeks at least a partial *tikkun* (repair) of the world, while simultaneously asking questions of both the divine and human covenantal partners. Memory, however, is paradoxical. For example, on the political level the author observes that memory can be both a "sanctuary" and an "abomination." Wiesel notes that the reason people in Bosnia hate each other is because they "remember what happened to their parents or their sisters or their grandparents" (Wiesel and Heffner 2001, 145). Theologically, God Himself needs to be reminded of Auschwitz. For survivors as well, memory is a two-edged sword. Issahar the scribe, in Wiesel's vignette "The Scrolls, Too, Are Mortal," embodies this paradox (Wiesel 1979b, 96). He observes that memory is both "our real kingdom" and "a graveyard."

The concept of memory permeates all of Wiesel's novels but is especially central in *The Forgotten*. Yet Wiesel's response to an interviewer concerning the possibility of imposing survivors' memory on those who follow illuminates his notion of the paradox of memory. On the one hand, he believes that anyone who listens to a witness becomes a witness. "All who listen to our tale," he attests, "become custodians of that tale" (Wiesel and Heffner 2001, 154). On the other hand, Wiesel terms the imposition of survivor memory "a terrible dilemma." While he would like us to remember, Wiesel knows the limitations of memory. He himself claims to remember selectively. This claim refers to those victims of the Shoah whom he has not gathered in his memory. The author views his task as bringing his listeners "closer to the gate" of memory (Wiesel and Heffner 2001, 155).

Postmemory and the Second Generation

Throughout Wiesel's writings the author privileges survivor memory. Only those who experienced the kingdom of night have a memory of the horrors of the death camps. Only those who were there know what it means to be, in Primo Levi's words, "on the bottom." Further, the survivors' experience has theological ramifications. Wiesel contends that in addition to God's name being ineffable, so, too, is the survivors' ordeal during the Shoah. Consequently, the central paradox of memory for Wiesel is that while survivors must bear witness, they know that the reality of the death camps lies beyond comprehensive articulation. Survivors must continually shoulder the responsibility to remember, knowing that this task in its fullness remains impossible.

More than three decades ago Wiesel began exploring the psychosocial and theological impact of postmemory on the second generation. This exploration coincided with an increased societal recognition of the second generation as a distinct group, and with the appearance of novels and films written by sons and daughters of survivors. Further, the issue of trauma studies was also beginning to come into scholarly focus.

Although he does not use the term "postmemory" in any of his second-generation novels, *The Oath* (1973), *The Testament* (1981), *The Fifth Son* (1985b), and *The Forgotten* (1992) collectively form an extended midrash on the nature of this generation's Holocaust memory and how it shapes second-generation Jewish identity. Tellingly, there is a clear evolution of the protagonists' ability to receive and transmit this memory. Inheriting the traumatic experience of his survivor parents, the nameless son portrayed in *The Oath* (1973) is overwhelmed and contemplates suicide. Over thirty years have passed since Wiesel wrote of the protagonist, "He arouses our pity because he doesn't even have the consolation of being a witness. He represents all my students and all the young people who are so perplexed" (Edelman 1978, 18).

Second-generation postmemory in *The Oath* reveals a sense of helplessness. Wiesel observes of this generation, "Born after the Holocaust, you have inherited the burden but not the mystery. And you were told: Go ahead, do something with it." The son is unable to communicate with his mother, who herself suffers the trauma of having lost her firstborn son in the Holocaust. Yet the protagonist's life is saved by Azriel ("whom God helps"), the sole survivor of a pre-Holocaust conflagration in the village of Kolvillag ("every village" or "the entire world"). Breaking his vow of silence about the pogrom, Azriel tells the youth what occurred so many years earlier. Azriel's testimony saves the youth's life and compels him to tell the tale. Further, it reveals the ongoing dialogue between speech and silence in the author's work. Specifically concerning the second generation, Ellen Fine writes, "this child of survivors is the listener who, in turn, becomes the narrator—the person responsible for transmitting the book. He is . . . the inheritor of the testimony" (Fine 1982, 130).

Postmemory in *The Testament*, which is set primarily in Russia, concerns a mute witness. Grisha, a diminutive of Gershon (Gershonites were identified with both the Tabernacle and the Jerusalem Temple), intentionally bites off his own tongue in order to avoid betraying his imprisoned father. Paltiel ("God is my refuge"/"I am a refugee from God") is a poet imprisoned by Stalin. Paltiel, who had rejected Judaism and wandered through Europe, where, among other things, he witnessed a death camp, writes a testament that, in fact, is an act of penance. He is a *ba'al teshuva*, a returner to the faith. The testament recounts the historical suffering of the Jewish people, rejects communism ("Godless messianism"), and affirms *ahavat Israel* (love of Israel). Following Paltiel's murder, his manuscript is smuggled out of prison by Zupanev, a stenographer and night watchman.

Zupanev serves as a father substitute and tutor to Grisha. Responding to his own query about who will tell the tale when the witnesses have been murdered, the stenographer tells the youth, "Each generation shapes its own truth." Wiesel's novel eloquently captures the paradoxical dynamics of postmemory. On the one hand, Grisha's muteness symbolizes the inability of the second-generation witnesses to speak about the Shoah. On the other hand, Grisha embraces the mission of this generation in musing, "my father is a book and books do not die." Grisha goes to Israel on the eve of the Yom Kippur War, where he bears witness for his father by becoming his scribe. As Fine observes, "Like the other surviving sons in Wiesel's works, Grisha's task is to preserve the continuity of history and the autonomy of the Book." Speaking, notes Fine, "is clearly less important here than the vow to remember" (144).

The Fifth Son, set primarily in America, represents a crucial departure in Wiesel's portrayal of second-generation postmemory. On the one hand, the author himself assumes the voice of a second-generation member in portraying the transmission of trauma. Further, he describes a survivor who wishes to forget the Shoah. Reuven ("see, a son") is a survivor whose life has been truncated by the Holocaust. As Charlotte Wardi writes, he "n'a pas voulu 'ṥpéarer les vivant des morts' " (Wardi 1996, 137). Preoccupied and melancholy, Reuven has little interaction with his son. Instead he writes letters to Ariel, his firstborn son murdered in the Shoah. His American-born son is also named Ariel. This name itself symbolizes the ambiguity of post-Holocaust Judaism. Ariel can be translated both as "lion" or "mountain of God," and it may also denote the destruction of Jerusalem.

The American-born Ariel speaks for the second generation in observing, "I suffer from an event I have not even experienced." He, like *The Oath*'s anonymous protagonist, is a second "only" son. Lacking access to his parents—Ariel's mother is institutionalized, unable to cope with the murder of her child—the protagonist seeks to gain postmemory through a variety of sources. He speaks to his father's two survivor friends, Bontchek and a kabbalist named Simha the Dark. Further, he reads voraciously about the Holocaust, although Wiesel observes that "novels, essays, and films cheapen the experience." Moreover, he goes on a pilgrimage to Reshastadt ("evil city") in Germany in order to confront the Nazi who murdered his brother. Reuven mistakenly believes that he had killed the Nazi after the war.

Wiesel's novel juxtaposes memory of the Holocaust and the Passover Haggadah. As the national memory of salvation assumed its role in the religious and ritual life of the Jewish people, so too must survivor memory "fuel the imagination" of the second generation. In addition to the four sons of the traditional Haggadah, the simple, the wicked, the wise, and the child, there is now a fifth son. This is the one murdered in the Shoah. The *presence of the absent ones* is palpable. As the Haggadah, whose root meaning is *l'haggid* (to tell), commands Jews to tell the tale of Passover, the Holocaust issues its own command. Just as it is the father's duty to teach his son the tale of the Exodus from Egypt, so too is it Reuven's duty to tell Ariel of Auschwitz. Reuven's unwillingness to assume this role leads Simha to remind his reclusive friend that a father's obligation is to tell the tale to his son. The adult Ariel becomes a college professor, in which context he will share his own Holocaust postmemories while helping shape those of succeeding generations.

The Forgotten and Postmemory—Possibilities and Limitations

Wiesel's emphasis on the importance of the second-generation witness reaches its apogee with the appearance of *The Forgotten*. Unlike the earlier novels of this genre, the relationship between survivor experience and second-generation imagination is richly portrayed. Elhanan and Malkiel engage in frequent dialogues. Further, the rituals of acquiring postmemory are described in great detail, from Malkiel's listening to survivor testimony to his making a European pilgrimage to Elhanan's birthplace and to the grave of his martyred grandfather. Moreover, *The Forgotten* is a literary expression of Wiesel's understanding of the task of the second generation. Sons and daughters of survivors, he attests, have a specific mission. Their task is to "keep the [survivors'] tale alive—and sacred" (Wiesel 1985c, 321). Consequently, memory itself bears great theological significance.

Fathers and Sons

The relationship between Elhanan and Malkiel is more fully developed than in any of Wiesel's previous second-generation novels. The father and son engage in dialogue on topics such as theology and politics. In fact, *The Forgotten* recalls Wiesel's understanding that it is the son's obligation to continue his father's story. First articulated in his classic memoir *Night* (1982b), this obligation now assumes increased intensity. Unlike *The Fifth Son*'s Reuven, Elhanan wishes to remember. But cannot. Before being stricken by his disease, Elhanan willingly assumes his paternal role, which Wardi describes as follows: "C'est elle qui soude la chaîne qui relie les Juifs à

Dieu. Afin qu'elle ne se brise, les pères doivent enseigner aux fils l'Histoire de leur peuple, celle de l'Alliance entre le Seigneur et leurs ancêtres" (Wardi 1996, 131).

The relationship between father and son is one of caring, concern, and love. Malkiel is with his father on Shabbat and other Jewish holy days, and visits him often. Further, Elhanan teaches his son Talmud, and the two frequently study together. On the symbolic level this relationship also stands for Wiesel's ideal vision of the relationship between survivors and the second generation. In this vision, the second generation takes up the torch of memory and carries it forward in a world that to a large extent is either indifferent or hostile to memory. But children of survivors have the added obligation of being "exiled from a world that has ceased to exist, that has been violently erased" (Hirsch 1997, 243). Consequently, postmemory must deal with the issue of reclaiming an absent memory.

Rituals of Memory

Earlier, I referred to *The Forgotten*'s central question: can there be a memory transfusion? Elhanan muses, "Is it not a father's duty to help his son remember, to magnify his past, to enrich his memory?" In order to more fully transfuse this memory, the father sends Malkiel on a mission: the son must visit Feherfalu ("White Village"), the Romanian town of his father's birth. "You'd understand me better," attests Elhanan, "you'd remember more." This ritual of pilgrimage in the second generation is an attempt to familiarize themselves with the "landscape of memory." Memory is related to a physical space. In Feherfalu, Malkiel visits the grave of his grandfather, for whom he is named. His words, offered as a prayer, beseech the grandfather to intercede in heaven to restore Elhanan's health.

Specifically concerning the issue of memory transfusion, Malkiel has two sources. He listens to his father's testimony with ritual intensity, tape-recording Elhanan's stories so as not to miss a single detail, and meets two survivors in Feherfalu. Wiesel writes of the transfusion process in spatial terms: "In proportion as Elhanan felt his memory diminish, Malkiel felt his own expand." Yet the son meditates on the second generation's dilemma. Praying before his grandfather's grave, Malkiel attests that "It is the son's duty not to let his father die." However, he also knows that while he can bear witness on behalf of Elhanan, he also states, "Forgive me, Father. There is no such thing as a memory transfusion. Yours will never become mine." While Elhanan has brought Malkiel "closer to the gates," the second generation takes in only "fragments of memory" and wonders if that is enough.

Malkiel's acquisition of Holocaust postmemory is enhanced by his encounters with Feherfalu's only two remaining Jews, Hershel the gravedigger and Ephraim. Hershel tells the youth about the Great Reunion, a conclave of long deceased pious rabbis who gather in Feherfalu's cemetery to ponder how they may help the town's besieged Jews. Hershel's tale underscores the author's long held conviction that all events in Jewish history are related. The gravedigger also relates the tale of Malkiel's grandfather's martyrdom during the Shoah, and the fact that Hershel himself had assassinated the leader of the local anti-Semites, thus emphasizing that Jews both spiritually and physically resisted Nazism.

Malkiel's encounter with the blind Ephraim provides the novel's most dramatic portrayal of the possibilities and limitations of memory transfusion. Wiesel writes, "The blind man leaned toward Malkiel as if to inspect him; their heads touched. The old man's breath entered Malkiel's nostrils." This depiction conjures Michelangelo's *The Creation of Adam*, which portrays the hand of God giving life to the first human being. Yet there is a crucial difference. Michelangelo's deity vivifies creation. Ephraim, for his part, articulates the difference between survivors and the second generation. "Feel the chill of my hand," he says, and adds, *"go home"* (emphasis added). Memory is thus both bond *and* barrier. Ephraim's post-Auschwitz *Amidah* prayer is uttered to a God whose justice is clouded. But the survivor—who contends, "I am memory"—reminds God that memory is more precious than sight.

The Forgotten as Wiesel's Prayer

For Wiesel literature and prayer are indivisible (Wiesel 1982c, 166–67). Consequently, *The Forgotten* may be read as a book of prayers. The novel opens with Elhanan's prayer; it also contains Ephraim's prayer and those of Malkiel. These prayers echo Wiesel's view that memory makes its ubiquitous claim on both God and humanity. For example Elhanan's prayer deepens Wiesel's fundamental question, *What of God in all this?* The survivor prays, "You well know, You, source of all memory, that to forget is to abandon, to forget is to repudiate. Do not abandon me, God of my fathers, for I have never repudiated You."

Yet the God who listens is also a complicit deity. Wiesel reverses the classical Shema, in which Israel is commanded to listen to God. Here, God is commanded to listen. And to remember: "God of Auschwitz, know that I must remember Auschwitz. And that I must remind You of it. God of Treblinka, let the sound of that name make me, and You, tremble now and always. God of Belzec, let me, and You, weep for the victims of Belzec."

The Forgotten poignantly reveals the fact that the loss of a parent's memory echoes among members of the next generation who are deprived of this memory. Alzheimer's disease threatens to break the chain of Jewish and Holocaust memory transmission. It is Wiesel's prayer that the second generation will take up the torch of remembrance. Moreover, bearing witness has theological resonance. For instance, a midrash has God tell the Jewish people: "You are my witnesses, says the Lord"—that is, "if you are My witnesses, I am God, and if you are not My witnesses, I am, as it were, not God" (Midrash Psalms, on 123:1). In the case of postmemory, Malkiel is the spokesperson for Wiesel's prayer. "Whatever happens," pledges the young man, "I will have to justify my father's faith in me. He made me his messenger; I will have to prove myself worthy of his message." Yet the novel ends on an ambiguous note. Elhanan, who knows that what is not transmitted is forever lost, can say no more.

Wiesel, like Job of antiquity, knows that while there is every reason in the world to despair, it is his duty to reject despair. Grappling with the elusive content of an unmasterable and unprecedented trauma, the author nevertheless utilizes the biblical and haggadic injunctions to "Tell Thy Son." Yet he expands these precepts, investing the second-generation witnesses with a threefold mission: they must anchor their witness in survivor testimony, which in itself is sacrosanct; they must make a pilgrimage to the landscape of memory in order to deepen their understanding of family and national history; and they must, in turn, bear witness to their own children.

◆ *Memory and God* ◆

9

Augustine on God and Memory

PAULA FREDRIKSEN

ELIE WIESEL in both his literary work and his social activism has committed himself to recollection as a moral enterprise. In the private sphere created between his text and the reader, Wiesel explores his personal past to invoke the memory of charged presence—of loved ones, of lost worlds, of a silent God. In the public sphere of humanitarian activity, Wiesel holds those present accountable to the moral lessons of history, the communal past, creating from the memory of Jewish victimization an ethics of universal responsibility. In both endeavors, memory provides the matter for moral reflection.

Wiesel's ability to put his own, profoundly Jewish experience in service to his larger philosophical and ethical vision gives his writing its poignancy and power. In so doing, he follows a tradition in Western letters that goes back at least as far as the fourth century, to the work of the profoundly Catholic bishop Augustine of Hippo. In 397, looking back over the external events and drastic inner reorientations that had ruptured his own past, Augustine composed his uniquely original work of autobiographical philosophy, the *Confessiones*.[1] By investigating

---

1. The most recent scientific text of the *Confessiones*, together with a commentary encompassing a tremendous range of secondary works, may be found in O'Donnell (1992). I use here the English translation of Chadwick (1991).

the structure and argument of this work, we can see how the reflections of another introspective, religiously sensitive thinker, at a completely different cultural and historical moment, also put memory at the juncture between past self and present self, and at the juncture between Self and God.

. . .

The *Confessiones* has been called the first introspective autobiography in history, and in one sense this is so. Constructed as a prayerful address to God, the work opens with speculations about who or what Augustine was even before birth, through birth ("from the parents of my flesh, him from whom and her in whom You formed me in time," 1.6, 7) and early education, up through the death of his mother Monica in 387 shortly after his conversion to Catholicism (9.13, 36). But once we conclude our reading of book 9, the final narratively autobiographical section, we have some 40 percent of Augustine's story still to go: book 10, on memory; book 11, on eternity and time; book 12, on material and spiritual creation; book 13, on revelation and time's end. Augustine may be using his past to make his points, but clearly he has more than autobiography in mind.

I find it more helpful to regard the *Confessiones* as a sort of meditative triptych, conceived around the problem of how the individual,

---

Parts of the present discussion draw on two of my earlier essays, Fredriksen (2000b), "Patristic *Pramā* and *Pramāṇa*," and Fredriksen (2000a), "Allegory and Reading God's Book." Those interested in a closer consideration of the dynamics of retrospection and knowledge in the *Confessiones* might consult the fine essay "Augustine: Reason and Illumination," by R. A. Markus (1970). Peter Brown's now-classic biography, *Augustine of Hippo*, has a valuable discussion of the autobiographical aspects of the *Confessiones* (1967, 146–81).

trapped in time, can know the eternal God. Its triple structure recapitulates its theme, for the three uneven "panels" of Augustine's presentation have as their subject, respectively, the Past (books 1–9, his retrospect on events from 354 to 387), the Present (books 10 and 11, on memory and the nature of time), and the Future (books 12 and 13, on the beginning and, thus, the end of time). The argument of the whole rests on the central argument of the central "panel": that memory is necessary not simply for recollection, but also for cognition and perception. It is through the exercise of his or her memory that the individual—time-bound, imperfect, mortal—is enabled to know and to recognize both him/herself and, most especially, Truth. Truth for Augustine relates immediately and necessarily to God—not the God of the philosophers, toward which all this self-conscious speculation might seem to tend; but the God of Abraham, Isaac, and Jacob, the God of the Bible, the God who created and pronounced his creation good. Put simply: Memory is the site of our illumination. Memory is our bridge to the world outside ourselves, to ourselves, and to God.

How does man find God? He turns first to God's creation, his mighty works: God made them, but is not of them.

> What is the object of my love? I asked the earth and it said, "It is not I." I asked all that is in it; they made the same confession. I asked the sea, the deeps, the living creatures that creep, and they responded, "We are not your God. Look beyond us." . . . I asked heaven, sun, moon, stars; they said, "Nor are we the God you seek." And I said to all these things, "Tell me of my God who you are not; tell me something about him." And with a great voice they cried out, "He made us." *Confessiones*, 10.6, 9

Having exhausted external possibilities, Augustine then turns inward, to the soul. He ranges past the vital force his soul shares in common with animals, past the consciousness through which they and he process sense perception, until at last he reaches a place uniquely human, "the fields and vast palaces of memory" (10.8, 12). And it is from here that Augustine sees the way that man is made most truly in God's image, for human thought, human memory, is purely nonmaterial. The memory of an object displaces no volume. Mental life, like God, is purely spiritual. Indeed, the vastness and power of memory—"a spreading limitless room within me"— overwhelms Augustine. Memory is the seat of human self-transcendence, despite being that part of the soul where the individual is most deeply his or her individual self. "Who can reach memory's utmost depth? Yet it is a faculty of my soul and belongs to my nature. In fact, I cannot totally grasp all that I am. The mind is not large enough to contain itself" (10.8, 15). In both its utter nonmateriality and in its self-transcendence, human memory is an indwelling analogy of God.

More than a warehouse of images and past feelings, memory also serves an essential cognitive function: it is the seat of a priori knowledge (such as mathematical principles and other kinds of abstract thought [10, 17; 12, 19]). The mind, through memory, *recognizes* truth. When such truths were formulated for him, asks Augustine, "how did I recognize them and say, 'Yes, that is true'? The answer must be that they were already in my memory, but remote and pushed back ... as if in most secret caverns" (10, 17). Through memory, too, language is processed, because the sounds of words only signify the things to which they point (in this case, ideas without sense-referents), yet Augustine had understood them. The Augustinian *memoria* thus functions in much the same way as the Platonic *anamnesis*, though whereas in the pagan system this capacity points toward the life of the soul before its existence in the body, for Augustine it points to a preconscious intuition of the mind, implanted through Christ, on account of which the soul instinctively yearns to know God, the ultimate object of its love. In this last sense, memory provides the readiest analogy to the sort of unmediated apprehension by which God knows us, and with which humans, eschatologically, will know both themselves and God: "When I remember memory, my memory is present to itself by itself" (16, 24).

Yet animals, too, have memory. Human knowledge of God calls for something even greater. Accordingly, Augustine urges himself onward, inward, upward: What am I to do now, O my true life, my God? I shall mount beyond this power of memory, I shall mount beyond it, and come to you, O lovely light. . . . I shall pass beyond memory to find you: but where will I find you? If I find you beyond my memory, then I shall be without memory of you. And how will I find you if I am without memory of you?" (17, 26).

An indwelling memory of God, through which the soul's innate desire for happiness orients it toward God, may go back, Augustine conjectures, to humanity's primal parents (20, 29). With this allusion to Adam, Augustine invokes, as well, the Fall, for he identifies Adam as "that man who first sinned, in whom we all died." From this point on, Augustine's meditation grows increasingly elegiac, and the themes of the ubiquity and subtlety of sin, of the moral ambiguity of sexual desire experienced in sleep, of the dangerous manyness into which the soul, slipping into love of creature rather than Creator, can dissipate itself, sound increasingly. Hence, argues Augustine, the necessity of sexual continence that God commands, "for by continence we are collected and bound up into unity within ourselves, whereas we had been scattered abroad in multiplicity" (29, 40).

Memory as now constituted was called into existence by sin, because sin—historically, Adam's; existentially, everyone's—separates man from God. But sin affected the divine/human relationship in a way that was, itself, precisely historical: after Adam, humanity was sunk into a new experience of *time* and, thus, of perception, most especially vis-à-vis the divine. God continued transcendent and outside time; humanity's entire existence became temporally conditioned. Knowledge, most especially knowledge of God, which was once immediate and unmediated, changed as man's soul, after the Fall, became itself distended in time, fraught with disunity.

The nature of time itself, Augustine maintains, underscores and feeds this distension. Time is a psychological function: it exists within the soul. While we speak of time as Past, Present, and Future, only the middle term has any "being" or reality. The Past no longer exists; the Future does not yet exist. The present alone is. Yet of what duration is the present? Reflection reveals that the present itself is an ungraspable, elusive *punctum*. All of man's consciousness, his memory, his entire ability to grasp truth exists within and is circumscribed by the present, a razor-thin slice of reality suspended between two infinitely receding types of nonbeing, Past and Future.

> Not even one day is entirely present. All the hours of the day add up to twenty-four. The first of them has the others in the future, the last has them in the past.... A single hour is itself constituted of fugitive moments.... If we can think of some bit of time which cannot be divided into even the smallest instantaneous moments, that alone is what we call "present." And this time flies so quickly from the future into the past that it is an interval with no duration. Any duration is divisible into past and future: the present occupies no space. (11.15, 20)

This distension in time constitutes the great measure of difference and distance between our mode of consciousness and God's. God, in eternity, knows all things simultaneously, as do the angels who dwell in the "heaven of heavens," the "intellectual, nonphysical heaven where the intelligence's knowing is a matter of simultaneity—not in part, not in an enigma, not through a glass, but complete total openness, face to face. . . . concurrent, without any temporal successiveness" (12.13, 16). God is not in time.

Man's existence in time affects the nature both of experience and of language. Time constantly, literally, rushes by him, too swift and atomized to process: man's experience—by definition, solely of the present—constantly runs between the fingers of his soul like sand. Meaning is distilled only retrospectively, through the integrative functioning of memory: it is only in recollection that the person can actually understand what he has experienced and see true meaning in it. By making this argument at the close of his book, Augustine thus teaches us to see, retrospectively, the point of his autobiographical narrative in the first nine books: he understood the meaning of all those events—stealing the pears, reading Cicero, joining the Manichees, quitting Africa for Italy, listening to Ambrose—not as he was living them, but only retrospectively from the vantage point of his conversion, once God had revealed himself to him. His closing arguments teach us that, epistemologically, this was the only way he could have understood his experience—that is, once his memory, "the stomach of the mind" (10.14, 22), had done its digestive work.

Language itself is tangled up in time, distended and thus itself intrinsically narrative, dependent on the linear passage from being (present) to nonbeing (past) before it can be understood. Consonants and vowels alternate to create phonemes, words follow words, nouns verbs, until we get to the end of a sentence, remember the whole, and so understand what this unit of sound has meant to convey. (Like all ancient people, Augustine thinks of words and texts orally, in terms of their being spoken and heard; compare 11.7, 9.) Memory is the means of the soul's contact with time, since memory, to function, functions only in the present. Meaning is thus necessarily mediated—through memory, images, signs, words. And just as time is not the same as the units we measure it by, so meaning is not the same as those words we use in our attempts to convey it.

This mediation is true even of scripture, God's word, conveyed as it is through the signs of contingent languages. Though divine revelation, scripture itself is infinitely interpretable (12.23, 32), capable of sustaining a diversity of truths whose validity cannot be limited by the historically contingent intentions of their original authors (12.23, 32–30, 41). Scripture mediates knowledge of God; it bridges time and eternity. But since it (necessarily) describes God through narrative, it measures the difference between God and us:

> O man [Augustine imagines God explaining to him], what my scripture says, I say. Yet scripture speaks in time-conditioned language [*temporaliter dicit*], and time does not touch my Word, existing with me in an equal eternity. So I see those things which through my Spirit you see, just as I also say those things which through my Spirit you say. Accordingly, while your vision of them is temporally determined, my seeing is not temporal; just as you speak of these things in temporal terms, but I do not speak in the successiveness of time [*non ego temporaliter dico*]. (13.29, 44)

Love of truth, knowledge of God, true perception of self and other mediated through memory, available through personal recollection made public through the written word—these convictions motivated Augustine's *Confessiones*; they shape as well the work of Elie Wiesel. In honor of my colleague and his work, I have tried to share with you some of the grand themes that contour Augustine's.

10

God's Memory

NEHEMIA POLEN

DOES GOD HAVE A MEMORY? Why of course, we are tempted to respond; in fact, God has a perfect memory. But a moment's reflection reveals how problematic such a notion would be. For to have a perfect memory—presumably because past, present and future are all the same for a Being existing in an eternal now—is to have no memory at all, since one does not remember the moment we call now, one simply lives in it. Perfect memory self-destructs into incoherence.

The Bible knew better than that. It endows God with a memory, but not a perfect one. God remembers Noah in the ark, but when he makes a covenant with Noah, he provides himself with a visual aid: "I have set my bow in the cloud, and it shall be for a sign of the covenant between me and the earth. And it shall come to pass, when I bring clouds over the earth, and the bow is seen in the cloud, that I will remember my covenant" (Gen. 9:13–15). So the rainbow jogs God's memory. It is a kind of arched string around the divine finger. Using the same terms, *ot brit*—sign of the covenant—God provides another visual sign, that of circumcision, for his covenant with Abraham. And sometimes God writes notes to himself, a list of names to cherish and remember, worn on the garments of his special assistant. In Exodus 28:29 we read that "Aaron shall carry the names of the children of Israel in the breastplate of judgment on his heart when he goes in to the holy place, for remembrance before the Lord continually."

It is not only catching God's eye that assists divine recall; auditory reminders also play a role. In Numbers 10:10 we read, "On the day of your joy, and on your festivals, and on your new moon days, you shall blow with trumpets over your burnt and peace offerings, and they shall be to you for a reminder (*le-zikaron*) before your God." Most significantly, when God remembers the Children of Israel after many years of bondage, it is an acoustic phenomenon that calls them to mind. "And it came to pass in the course of those many days that the king of Egypt died; and the children of Israel sighed by reason of the bondage, and they cried, and their cry came up to God from their bondage. And God heard their groaning, and God remembered his covenant with Abraham, with Isaac, and with Jacob" (Exod. 2:23–24).

Given this evidence that divine memory needs jogging, it is not surprising that those who beseech God are often anxious about securing their place in His memory. Thus Hannah in her prayer for a son says, "O Lord of hosts . . . if you will remember me and not forget your maidservant, but will give thy handmaid a man child, then I will give him to the Lord all the days of his life" (I Samuel 1:11), and indeed, when the narrator announces that her wish was granted we are told, "and the Lord remembered her" (*va-yizkereha*) (v. 19). How fitting, then, that in the synagogue, this chapter of First Samuel is read on Rosh Hashanah, New Year's Day, the Day of Judgment, known in the Pentateuch as *zikhron teruah* (Lev. 23:24)—the day of memory, of sounding the horn, perhaps the day of sounding the horn to evoke memory.

Part of the task of the biblical prophet is to remind God of his promises. After the episode of the golden calf Moses pleads, "Remember Abraham, Isaac, and Jacob your servants" (Exod. 32:12). In the face of Israel's sins and the looming threat of God's wrath, the prophet intercedes by evoking the memories of the beloved patriarchs and the promises made to them. Indeed, every true prophet of Israel must be willing to confront God's anger, challenging him to arouse the compassionate side of his nature.[1] It is in this spirit of prophetic intercession that we read Habakkuk's poignant plea to God, "in wrath, remember mercy" (3:2).

The Bible knows the terrible truth that "in the day of his anger [the Lord] did not remember his footstool [=the Sanctuary]" (Lam. 2:1). So the greatest consolation that the prophets offer Israel is that God does indeed remember them. Dovetailed between Jeremiah's dire warnings and withering critiques of Israel are the tender words of assurance that God has not forgotten the earlier, happier days of their relationship: "Thus saith the Lord: I remember for your benefit the affection of your youth, the love of your espousals; how you went after me in the wilderness, in a land that was not sown" (Jer. 2:2). And among the images of glorious restoration and salvation at the end of the book of Isaiah, we find that God has set watchmen on the walls of Jerusalem to remind him constantly of his promises to the city: "Ye that are the Lord's remembrancers, take ye no rest, and give [the Lord] no rest, till he establish, and till he make Jerusalem a praise in the earth" (Isa. 62:6–7).[2]

The biblical figure who displays the most anxiety about God's memory and his place in it is Nehemia. Nehemia asks God to remember him, four times: "Remember me, my God, for good, according to all that I have done for this people" (Neh. 5:19); "Remember me

---

1. On this theme, see Muffs 1992, 9–48.
2. See note of Slotki 1961, 303.

o my God, concerning this, and wipe not out my good deeds that I have done for the house of my God" (13:14); "Remember me, o my God, concerning this also, and spare me according to thy abundant love" (13:22); and finally, the very last words in the book, "Remember me, o my God, for good" (13:31). What is the source of this incessant concern for God to remember him? Moses asked God to remember the patriarchs and the covenant, but never did he ask God to remember his own good deeds, even when he pleaded with God to be allowed to enter the Promised Land.

The rabbis of the Talmud disapprove of Nehemia's imploring God to remember him, seeing it as evidence of pride and self-satisfaction (Sanhedrin 93b), but I would like to cast a more favorable light on this aspect of his character. The book of Nehemia (originally one work with the book of Ezra) is among the latest books of the biblical canon, along with Chronicles, Daniel, and Esther. These Second Temple works display certain commonalities of language and theological approach (as well as significant differences).[3] For our purposes here it is important to note that while God manifests his will, presence, and power quite openly in the early books of the Bible, as we move forward through the Tanakh there is a gradual receding of the divine presence, a "hiding of the face."[4] By the time we reach the Persian period and the books that emerge from that era, God plays little or no overt role. As many have observed, he does not appear at all in the book of Esther. The situation in Nehemia, while less extreme, is similar. God never makes an appearance in the book, nor is he explicitly heard from. Nehemia frequently invokes God's name and prays—indeed his prayers are inspiring and exemplary—but in the book we are never told God's response in

---

3. See Talmon 1987, 357–64.
4. See Friedman 1995, 207–22; cf. Miles 1995.

words. Nehemia succeeds in his plans to rebuild Jerusalem and to reform the religious life of the people, but the question of whether his success is owing to divine providence or to Nehemia's courage, leadership, and diplomatic skills is never resolved.[5] In earlier books of the Bible, the prophetic word or the voice of the narrator makes it clear where God's sympathies lie, but neither is heard in the Nehemia memoir.

Nehemia was, according to his self-description, a man who came to seek the welfare of the Children of Israel; he attributes the origin of his plans, he tells us, to "what God put in my heart to do for Jerusalem" (2:12). But surely he knew, and he knew that others well understood, that there was no proof that his plans were the result of divine inspiration. When he rebukes the nobles for their exploitation of the poor, he says, "then I consulted with myself" (5:7). In the end, his book and his entire project—the foundation for Second Temple Judaism—is his consultation with himself.

Prophets do not appear in the book of Nehemia, excepting false ones, who attempt to trick him into an action that would humiliate and discredit him (Neh. 6:10–14). When Nehemia institutes a census, he says, "and my God put it into my heart to gather together . . .

---

5. Nehemia is acutely aware at all times that he serves at the sufferance and pleasure of the Persian authorities, and that his plans would come to naught without their support. See Neh. 1:11–2:8. Even at the triumphant moment when the walls of Jerusalem have been built and the people enter into a solemn covenant to place the Torah at the center of their reconstituted life, Nehemia frankly acknowledges that they have no political independence, and are "servants this day" (9:36) to Persia. It is quite astonishing that at this moment of what should be supreme celebration, Nehemia underscores the subservience of the people and the land, which "yields much increase to the kings which you [=God] have set over us because of our sins; also they have power over our bodies, and over our cattle, at their pleasure, and we are in great distress" (9:37).

the people" (7:5), but when a family of priests of questionable lineage presents itself, wishing to partake of the priestly perquisites, Nehemia is forced to tell them that "they should not eat of the holy things until there would rise up a priest with Urim and Thummim" (7:64). Of course, that never did happen. Priests there were, they wore priestly vestments, but the oracular power of the Urim and Thummim described in Exodus was never restored.[6]

And there is yet a greater, more fundamental omission. The schematic design of both the desert tabernacle and Solomon's temple is that of a nested series of rectangles (outer rampart or screen, courtyard, sanctuary, holy of holies). The focal point of the entire system was the ark of the covenant with the tablets written "by God's finger" in the Inner Sanctum. Now the restored temple of Ezra and Nehemia had the gates, the courtyards, the altars, the offerings, and the holy of holies, but the ark of the covenant was missing. The rituals of atonement were enacted, the sacrifices were brought, but the center was empty.[7] What a hasidic master was many

---

6. The Talmud (b. Yoma 21b; cf. 39a–b) lists five features of the First Temple that were absent in the second; among these are the Urim and Thummim, and, significantly, the Shekhinah itself. In general, rabbinic sources see Second Temple Judaism as a time of self-acknowledged decline and self-imposed surrender of the trappings of spiritual power. Note, for example the statement in Yoma 39b that early in the Second Temple period (after the death of Simeon the Just), the priests refrained from using the Tetragrammaton when blessing the people; according to Rashi, this was because they felt they were unworthy *("she-lo hayu kedai")*.

7. The full significance of this fact is not always grasped. Why, indeed, was there nothing in the holy of holies? Why did the priests in the early, formative days of the Second Temple—when the religious and political situation was still inchoate and fluid—not simply make an ark and place it in the holy of holies? It is hard to imagine that the thought did not occur to them. The temptation would have been great to buttress their claims to legitimacy and continuity with the putative presence of

centuries later to call "the innermost point" was gone.[8] As a sensitive and insightful religious man, Nehemia must have wondered whether the whole enterprise was worth it, whether it was even justified, or whether perhaps the restored temple was but a lifeless reproduction, a copy of what once was but could not be again.

He wondered, but still he proceeded. As has been said of Lincoln, he took a guess in twilight. He knew his work would always be tentative, provisional, unfinished, and open to recision. Most trou-

---

the ark of Moses. Who would have gainsaid their assertion or challenged its authenticity? The fact that the priests and leaders of the Second Commonwealth oversaw the reestablishment of the Temple and its cult, but omitted the key element mandated by the Torah, must be seen as an extraordinary act of self-restraint, an acknowledgment of the limited, partial nature of their project of restoration. On the other hand, it also suggests a profound confidence in the ongoing covenantal relationship with God, which could dispense with even the most essential tangible artifacts if they were not available. Israel of the Second Commonwealth was the people that had so much confidence in God's ongoing love for them that they had the courage to reject ersatz substitutes for what had been lost, but which (they firmly believed) would one day be restored. Perhaps this is the meaning of the enigmatic verse in Jeremiah (3:16), "And it shall come to pass, when you are multiplied and increased in the land, in those days, saith the Lord, They shall say no more, 'the ark of the covenant of the Lord; neither shall it come to mind; neither shall they make mention of it; neither shall they miss it; neither shall it be made any more.' "

Our suggestion, then, is that the Judaism of the Second Temple was consciously constructed as a religion of absence, in line with the realities of political powerlessness (see previous note).

Hardly any writers have pointed to the absence of the ark as a remarkable fact. See, however, W. Jackson Bates (1970), who writes, "The Ark of the covenant was gone, and no one felt at liberty to try to replace it with a substitute." A most helpful discussion of the differences between the first and second "Houses" is that of Simon Rawidowicz (1974, 81–209). He insightfully points to the "second house" as an era of "limitation," but he does not explore the theme we have developed here.

8. I am referring to Judah Leib Alter of Gur; see Green 1996.

bling of all, he understood that by placing a written document—the Torah—at the center of the renewed faith of Israel (see Neh. 8–9), he was to some degree repudiating the religion of the First Temple at the very time he was working to remember and recapture it. For to remember in writing is to freeze, and to freeze is to extinguish and to eternalize at once.[9]

So Nehemia asks God, again and again, to remember him for good. He yearned for the divine voice of assurance but it was not forthcoming. In asking God to remember, he asks for confirmation of his life and his work. He consoles himself with the thought of God's memory, but he lives in a world of uncertainty where the wisdom of one's best intentions is imponderable, even in retrospect. He lives, in short, in our world. In some sense, he—along with Ezra—is the maker of it. We can well understand why he is anxious, and why he asks God to remember him for good.

Given this anxiety over God's memory, which is an inherent part of Nehemia's legacy to the Judaism that followed him, it is not surprising that the rabbinic prayer book, based on talmudic sources, both asserts that God remembers everything and yet implores God, again and again, to remember us and our loved ones.[10]

• • •

For the medieval Jewish philosophers with their abstract and conceptually austere view of the deity, there was less concern about God's memory than about divine foreknowledge, which seemed to rule out human freedom of will. In a famous passage in *Mishneh Torah*,

---

9. This point is made with particular elegance and force by Annie Dillard (1987, 70–71).

10. This is particularly apparent in the High Holiday liturgy; see below.

Maimonides asserts that the two are not contradictory: while God knows what is going to happen, humans are still free to choose, and they are responsible and accountable for their actions. But Maimonides makes no mention of divine memory. Evidently the notion of divine memory would carry a much more anthropomorphic coloration than does divine foreknowledge. Humans have memory but no foreknowledge—and perhaps that was enough to ensure that Maimonides would see memory as unworthy of God. Memory is a human function, not an abstract, impersonal one. It is an expression of personality, always relational, directed, volitional. Only a person can engage in the active, constructive, and creative activity we call memory.

The philosophical approach to Judaism soon provoked a reaction known as the Kabbalah. The kabbalists taught that along with the unknowable transcendent divinity referred to as Ein-Sof, divinity self-manifests in ten stages known as *sefirot*. In the view of the kabbalists, it is the realm of the sefirot that is the true referent of the God of the Bible, the God in whose image man is made, who knows joy and anger, love and disdain, who is anchored in the world of place and time. As the thirteenth-century kabbalist Rabbi Azriel of Gerona put it, "Ein-Sof is perfection, lacking nothing. But if you say that [the divine] operates in the infinite but has no power in the realm of finitude, you thereby diminish divine perfection" (Shatz 1997, 30).[11] Just as God's power is in the domain of the unbounded, so does it reach into boundedness and limitation. If you do not allow God to penetrate the world of limits and finitude, you actually limit his perfection.

---

11. Shatz 1997, 30; see also ibn Gabbai 1992, chap. 8, 1:17. Cf. Dan and Kiener 1986, 90.

It is this God who remembers—and who needs to be reminded.[12]

Here as elsewhere, the kabbalah combines aspects of neoplatonic thought with mythic elements of the Jewish tradition to breathe new life in the biblical image of God that had nearly succumbed to the rigorous constraints of medieval religious rationalism. The return to the personal God of the Bible is completed in the hasidic movement. Hasidism absorbed the entire legacy of Jewish thought, but embraced with special enthusiasm those early strata, the Bible and the rabbinic *aggadah*, which emphasize the personal nature of God, with whom one can relate in dialogue, who is deeply involved with human beings, their destiny, their problems and concerns.

The Hasidim understood that God, to be God, must be implicated in time. Rabbi Levi Yitzhak of Berditchev (1740–1809) comments on a verse in Habakkuk (a fragment of which we have already quoted), "revive thy work in the midst of the years, in the midst of the years make known; in wrath remember mercy" (3:2). He writes, "When Israel is suffering they cry out to God for mercy. At such a time, the individual in prayer must attach his thought and his prayer to God. In response, God attaches himself to them and shows compassion. This is what Habakkuk means when he says, "revive thy work in the midst of the years, in the midst of the years make known": that is, suffering takes place in time, for in the transtemporal realm there is no suffering, no agony at all. So we ask God to invest himself in time, to come to know temporality and suffering, and therefore to understand our situation as we experience it. Then,

---

12. Memory is generally associated with the *sefirah Yesod*. See Cordovero 1586, 23:7. In contrast, forgetting is usually associated with the *kelipot*, the forces of darkness. See Cordovero 1586, 23:21.

as the verse concludes, God—even in the midst of wrath—will remember compassion.[13]

For Levi Yitzhak, divine memory and divine compassion depend on God's vesting himself in time, and this vesting in turn depends on human prayer, which is human consciousness directing itself and binding itself to God.

It is worthwhile pausing to consider what Levi Yizhak might say to Nehemia, so anxious over whether God would remember him. In light of the teaching just presented, we might surmise that he would say something like this: If you wish to secure your place in God's memory, you must keep God in your heart and mind at all times, for the divine and human memories are mirror images of each other.

But beyond this mystical notion of God-consciousness, so characteristic of early Hasidism, there is a moral dimension as well, in which God's mind is not the mirror image of man's, but the inverse of it, the photographic negative of it. This concept emerges from a teaching of Rabbi Moshe Leib of Sassov (1745–1807), known as the "father of widows and orphans," who spent much of his life helping the needy and redeeming from prison people falsely accused of crimes.

There is a lengthy section of the Musaf liturgy for Rosh Hashanah called *"Zikhronot,"* or "memories," which begins "You, God, remember all the deeds done in the universe and you recall all the creatures fashioned since earliest times." Toward the end of this section, we find the phrase *ki zokher kol ha-nishkahot attah hu me-olam*—"for you, God, remember all things forgotten from time everlasting."

Rabbi Moshe Leib explains: God remembers all things forgotten, but the converse is also true: God forgets all things remembered.

---

13. Kedushat Levi on Exod. 2:25 (Parashat Shemot, s.v. *"o yevo'ar va-yar',"* p. 87 in the Jerusalem 1978 ed.)

Whatever we forget, God remembers; but whatever we remember, God forgets. Consider our mitzvot, our good deeds. If we remember them with pride and self-satisfaction, if we consider them our ticket to heaven or to a life of honor here on earth, then God forgets them. On the other hand, if we forget them, not claiming virtue for ourselves or special privilege in consequence of our good deeds, then God remembers those good deeds and cherishes them. Now consider our sins. If we forget them, if we forget the wrongs we have done, the harm we may have caused, if we feel no remorse, then God remembers. But if we remember our misdeeds, looking upon them with deep regret, actively working to make amends and to change ourselves for the better, then God forgets those misdeeds. So, Rabbi Moshe Leib concludes, truly is it said that God only remembers what we forget.[14]

In light of this teaching let us consider what Rabbi Moshe Leib might say to the biblical Nehemia. We can imagine him saying: Nehemia, you are anxious about God's remembering you for good? You wish to secure your place in history? Then give your achievements away. Surrender them as a gift to God and to your people. For the surest way to remove them from God's heart is to hold them with preciousness in your own.

・ ・ ・

This brief survey of sources points to a notion of God's memory as a social construct, an intergenerational armature of linkages anchored in moral commitment to communal stability and spiritual vision. But if God's memory is a social construct, then are we not, as

---

14. This teaching, originally an oral tradition, eventually found its way into twentieth-century hasidic anthologies, including Yeushson 1956, 26–27.

Ludwig Andreas Feuerbach said, making God (and his memory) in our image?

The Hasidim would say that this is the truth, but it is not the whole or final truth. For why do we wish to make God in our image, why are we capable of conceiving of such a God, if not for the fact that we indeed have the spark of the divine within us. We can only imagine transcendence because we are made in God's image, as Genesis told us long ago.

The hasidic texts on the reciprocity of memory thus far presented have focused largely on the mutual relationship between God and the individual of faith. But the biblical understanding of divine memory suggested by Nehemia moves from the individual to the collective, for Nehemia's entire project is the reestablishment and strengthening of his community and its sacred centers, especially Jerusalem and the Temple. Nehemia's own personal destiny is important only insofar as he subordinates it to the destiny of his people and respects its sacred ideals more than his own life.[15]

This communal dimension of divine memory is elegantly articulated by one of the boldest and most creative of all the hasidic masters, Rabbi Mordechai Yosef Leiner of Izbica (1801–1854), commenting on Malachi 3:16: "Then they who feared the Lord spoke to one another; and the Lord hearkened and heard it, and a book of remembrance was written before him for those who feared the Lord and took heed of his name." According to Rabbi Mordecai Yosef, the social setting of Malachi 3:16 is a group of friends who enjoy each others' company and who elevate their camaraderie by

---

15. See Neh. 6:11. On another occasion I hope to write about this verse and its theory of leadership, especially in comparison to the leadership model of Moses. The comparison focuses on Num. 20, especially 20:6.

directing it to a sublime purpose. When they meet they discuss matters of the spirit, giving and receiving advice on advancement in the service of God, sharing spiritual insight and wisdom. To the extent that these words of wisdom are embraced by the community of seekers, then they are inscribed in God's memory book. For, says Rabbi Mordechai Yosef, God's memory book is "the totality of the hearts of the Children of Israel."[16]

God's memory is a tapestry strung on the loom of human hearts.

. . .

Let us return once more to Nehemia, the royal cupbearer and advisor, religious reformer, builder, and governor of Judea. Or perhaps we should be less charitable and call him an activist or—most unkind of all—a politician. Did God remember him for good? We cannot presume to know the mind of God. All we do know is that the book of Nehemia was preserved and cherished as sacred scripture by the Jewish people. The canonization of the memoir is an implicit judgment on the man and his work. Ben Sira would later speak of Nehemia as one "whose memorial is great; who raised up for us the walls that were fallen, and set up the gates and bars, and raised up our homes again" (49:13). Nehemia's "remember me o my God for good" ends the penultimate book of the Hebrew Bible, and dovetails thematically with the last words of the last book of the Bible, Second Chronicles: "the Lord his God be with him, let him go up."[17] In light of the teaching of Rabbi Mordecai Yosef, we might say that Nehemia's concern to be remembered by God is not egotistical

---

16. Mei ha-Shilo'ah, Likkutei ha-Shas, Berakhot 11b, s.v. *Hitkinu* (in the Bnei Brak 1995 edition, this text is in 1:238).

17. On the connection between Ezra-Nehemiah and Chronicles, see Blenkinsopp 1988, 47–54.

self-indulgence, but a plea that the collective energies of his people should foster sacred ties of filiation, vectors pointing with quiet faith to a shared future.

In the end, the decision of the Jewish people has always been to rebuild after catastrophe, to resolve all doubts on the side of reconstruction and renewal, knowing full well that the effort to remember the past and to build for the future is the final confirmation of the irretrievability of the past—and still to go ahead.

God's memory is what impels us to action and buttresses our hopes in the face of the abyss. But God's memory is a meaningful concept only through the collective decision of the people to preserve memories as sacred, to cherish them, and, most importantly, to study and teach and transmit them.

To conclude: if God has a memory at all, it is because we give him ours.

But what, then, does God give us? The two things that make memory worth having: a vision of integrity and the courage to hope. And perhaps these two things are not so different from what a master teacher gives his students.

♦ *On Memory and the Holocaust* ♦

Afterword

ELIE WIESEL

I READ ALL THE TEXTS of this volume with both curiosity and gratitude. I felt enriched by their depth and moved by their warmth. For a teacher and a writer, there is no greater reward than being questioned and understood by one's peers.

Often I wonder: Have I sufficiently emphasized my doubts on our capacity to transmit what we have endured or received, memories of fear and fire, in words, just in words?

On the one hand, like Sisyphus, we keep on returning to the same events, each time hoping to elicit some painful yet necessary truth, both ancient and new, about a people's solitude, anguish, and death; then, having spoken, we realize that what had to be said remained, and perhaps had to remain, unsaid.

The old tension between the two obsessions of certain survivors has not disappeared in me. The duty to tell the tale is a powerful element in my life; but so is the realization that it cannot be told.

At times, I felt that it cannot be told not because the teller is unable to tell it, but because the listener cannot receive it. The language of what Yehiel Di-Nur called "another planet" is not the one used by people from this world. Language means a desire and an ability to communicate. Will ever a person who was not there understand what it meant to be there? Will that person penetrate the meaning of a statement that over there, on the other side of Creation, one was not afraid of death simply because we lived inside death?

And yet, the urgent obligation to bear witness remains constant. It is quite simple: a witness who does not give his or her testimony may be considered a false witness.

Don't we often hear orators reminding us that the wish of the dead was there to be told and their story to be transmitted? But what if, like in Kafka's writings, the tragedy of the messenger is that he cannot deliver the message?

I know and you know: countless books have been written, essays published on the general subject in many languages by philosophers and theologians, psychologists and scientists, historians and educators; I read most of them, fervently, forever eager to discover not something necessarily new but something profound and true, something that carries us back to those times of malediction and despair, something both unique and universal that allows or compels us to confront the darkness that enveloped God's world.

And each time I close one of the books I feel impoverished, saying to myself: "It's not it, no, it's not what I had hoped to find." Is it the fault of the author? Not really. I am grateful to all those teachers and writers who have the courage and the will to approach this burning chapter of our history, and are not afraid of losing, like the Sages who entered the Pardes, mind, faith, or life.

When the soul is in peril, one thinks of the Kotzker Rebbe, the great and awesome Reb Menahem-Mendel. He once said that some secrets of the Torah can only be communicated by some special words whereas others, more forbidden, can be transmitted only in silence. But there are also secrets that are so hidden, so deep and covered under so many layers, that even silence cannot express them.

Is that true of Holocaust experiences as well? Is it possible that, like God's true Name, they belong to the realm of the ineffable?

On the surface, at least, there are concrete, palpable reasons for such an approach. It has to do with the evil audacity of the Final Solution and its very magnitude. Thanks to our devoted historians and researchers we know quite a lot about it mainly from the murderers' viewpoint: captured documents, official and private letters, photographs, field reports enable us to learn of Hitler's "war against the Jews," a war he waged parallel to his war of conquest. We know who did what, when, where, and to whom. The decrees, the ghettos, the evacuations and deportations, the sealed cattle cars, the massacres, the death factories. Oh, yes, we acknowledge that, in those times, the killers taught Jews that there were endless ways of dying and so few of living.

And so we know what happened in hundreds of cities, villages, and hamlets. The extermination plan involved institutions of all the spheres of German society. Social scientists and chemists, architects and physicians helped implement it. The method was everywhere the same. Local anti-Semites were encouraged to stage a pogrom, thus creating an atmosphere of fear among Jews. Then came reassuring declarations from the German authorities. After every action, the surviving Jews were told that they were useful to the German war effort, thus safe. False promises preceded every new action. What happened in Warsaw, happened in Bialystok. The fate of Jewish Lublin was similar to that of Jewish Sighet. So much so that most stories sound alike. One has, at times, the feeling that everywhere one Jew, always the same, was murdered by one German, always the same, six million times. But, of course, it is the wrong way to approach testimony. There was an ontological aspect of every endeavor: each place had its own characteristic, its own human component, its own destiny. To know the real story of their deaths, we would need to know the individual death of each one of them. And we do not.

Oh, I know: I have written many books, on a variety of topics, in different forms. Novels, plays, portraits. . . . All have something in common: a commitment to memory. A loyalty to the dead.

In general, we know more about the perpetrators than about their victims. Can anyone who was not there feel what a prisoner in Treblinka felt? The terror of a selection in Auschwitz? The helplessness of a father or mother who sees their child thrown into the pit? The fear and trembling of a convoy heading East, destination unknown? In truth, it was easier for an Auschwitz inmate to imagine himself or herself free than for a free man or woman to imagine themselves in Auschwitz.

In one of his writings, Bertolt Brecht speaks to the reader: "You who will emerge from the flood in which we drowned, remember when you speak of our weaknesses the dark time from which you escaped."

And yet, some commentators, from a variety of disciplines, erected themselves as judges. During the Eichmann trial witnesses were asked, "Why didn't you resist?" Later, survivors were questioned: "How did you manage to survive?" In other words, "What did you have to do, meaning what bad things did you have to do so as to escape death?" Others, more compassionate, went to great length to explain to us how we felt, why we had chosen a certain path. In other words: like Job's friends who explained to him his ordeal, they explained to us Auschwitz and Buchenwald.

· · ·

On a quite different level, the witness is at times so frustrated that he or she is, perhaps subconsciously, moved to despair.

They look at the postwar world with its turbulence and turmoil, plagued by tragedy and hatred of all sorts, and they feel like howling with sadness and remorse: "What is happening to you? Haven't you heard our tales? Haven't we learned anything from our life and death? Have you been deaf and blind? Is that why the human condition hasn't improved?"

This was and remains a recurring leitmotif in my own adult life, as a writer, teacher, and social activist. Disillusioned, disenchanted, I fail to grasp the true implications of today's events. Things should have been much better.

For, strange as it may sound, in 1945, after the liberation, there was an element of hope in my despair. I said to myself: now society is compelled to head in a different direction. Never again will nations fight one another for a few miles; never again will hate dominate human relations; never again will there be racism, bigotry, fanaticism, and anti-Semitism. Never again will people dwell in a state of constant uncertainty and insecurity. Never again will children die of hunger, disease, and violence. Never again will innocent men, women, and children live in fear. Never again will humiliation be a national policy and murder a state philosophy.

And now, there is fear even in free societies. Travelers are conditioned to look at "the other" with suspicion. A few fanatic killers have changed many human attitudes.

And so, the witness-survivor is led to question himself or herself: is it perhaps our fault that the world remains unchanged? If two or three generations have ignored or rejected our message, could it be that it was poorly and inadequately handed down? Should we have chosen other words, another language to speak the unspeakable?

Which led me to approach the tragic case of writers who gave up on life. It is a fact that among those survivors who committed suicide, writers occupy the first place. The essayist Jean Améry, the poet Paul Celan, the novelists Jerzy Kosinski and Piotr Rawicz, the chroniclers Benno Wirzberg, Primo Levi, and Tadeus Borowski, the historian Josef Wulf. How can one not ask: why did they choose to die in Auschwitz after Auschwitz? Is it that they lost all hope either in the world or in themselves, in their own mission? Is it possible that having concluded that no words may ever express the memories, the images, the silent screams of the dead so as to change history, the writer-survivor felt useless and decided that life isn't worth living?

I know, these questions are meant to elicit pain.

And yet.

As I reread your essays, my good friends, I also feel gratitude.

Works Cited

• • •

Index

Works Cited

Augustine. 1991. *Confessiones.* Edited by Henry Chadwick. Oxford: Oxford Univ. Press.

Bates, W. Jackson. 1970. *The Burden of the Past and the English Poet.* Cambridge, Mass.: n.p.

Berger, Alan L. 1997. *Children of Job: American Second Generation Witnesses to the Holocaust.* Albany: State Univ. of New York Press.

Bergès, Michel. 1997. "Parce qu'il a signé beaucoup de documents, on fait de M. Papon un mythe politique." *Le Monde,* 22 Oct.

Bernstein, Michael-André. 1994. *Foregone Conclusions: Against Apocalyptic History.* Berkeley: Univ. of California Press.

Blenkinsopp, Joseph. 1988. *Ezra-Nehemiah.* Philadelphia: Westminster Press, 47–54.

Breton, André. [1928] 1960. *Nadja.* Translated by Richard Howard. New York: Grove Press.

Breznitz, Shlomo. 1971. "A Study of Worrying." *British Journal of Social and Clinical Psychology* 10:271–79.

———. 1993. *Memory Fields.* New York: Knopf.

Brown, Peter. 1967. *Augustine of Hippo.* Berkeley: Univ. of California Press.

Carjaval, Doreen. 1999. "Disputed Holocaust Memoir Withdrawn." *New York Times,* 14 Oct., B1.

Chambraud, Cécile. 1997. "Philippe Seguin accuse le gouvernement de vouloir gonfler la force électorale du Front national." *Le Monde,* 22 Oct.

Cohn, Dorrit. 1999. *The Distinction of Fiction.* Baltimore: Johns Hopkins Univ. Press.

Works Cited

Conan, Eric. 1997a. "Le casse-tête juridique." *L'Express*, 10 Oct.
———. 1997b. "Seize ans 'd'affaire Papon.' " *L'Express*, 2 Nov.
———. 1997c. "Un vichysto-résistant parmi d'autres." *L'Express*, 2 Oct.
———. 1998. *Le procès Papon: Un journal d'audience*. Paris: Gallimard.
Cordovero, R. Moses. 1586. *Pardes Rimmonim* 23:7.
Czech, Danuta. 1990. *Auschwitz Chronicle, 1939–1945. From the Archives of the Auschwitz Memorial and the German Federal Archives*. New York: Henry Holt.
Dan, Joseph, ed., and Ronald C. Kiener, trans. 1986. *The Early Kabbalah*. New York: Paulist.
Daniel, Jean. 1997. "Bouc émissaire et coupable." *Le nouvel observateur*, 13 Oct., 22.
Delacampagne, Christian. 1994. "L'Ombre de Vichy sur la littérature française: Entretien avec Jeffrey Mehlman." *Le Monde*, 23 Sept.
Dershowitz, Alan. 1995. Review of *The Hand That Signed the Papers*. *Jewish Advocate*, 20 July.
Dillard, Annie. 1987. "To Fashion a Text." In *Inventing the Truth: The Art and Craft of Memoir*, edited by William Zinsser, 70–71. Boston: Houghton Mifflin.
Doubrovsky, Serge. 1989. *Le livre brisé*. Paris: Grasset.
Dumay, Jean-Michel. 1997a. "Deux visions de l'histoire et de Vichy's opposent lors du procès Papon." *Le Monde*, 2 Nov.
———. 1997b. " 'Les préfets étaient des vice-rois qui régnaient dans les départements,' selon Jean-Pierre Azéma." *Le Monde*, 5 Nov.
———. 1997c. "Vichy avait transformé les citoyens en 'objets,' selon Philippe Burrin." *Le Monde*, 6 Nov.
———. 1997d. "Les derniers témoignages des partisans de Maurice Papon." *Le Monde*, 24 Oct.
———. 1998. "Michel Bergès élargit le champ des interrogations sur Maurice Papon." *Le Monde*, 22 Jan.
Dutourd, Jean. 1952. *Au bon beurre*. Paris: Gallimard.
Eakin, Paul John. 1985. *Fictions in Autobiography: Studies in the Art of Self-Invention*. Princeton, N.J.: Princeton Univ. Press.

Edelman, Lily. 1978. "A Conversation with Elie Wiesel." In *Responses to Elie Wiesel*, edited by Harry James Cargas. New York: Persea Books.

Einaudi, Jean-Luc. 1991. *La Bataille de Paris, 17 octobre 1961.* Paris: Seuil.

———. 1997. "Les mensonges de Maurice Papon." *Le Monde*, 25 Oct.

Eskin, Blake. 2002 *A Life in Pieces: The Making and Unmaking of Binjamin Wilkomirski.* New York: Norton.

Ezrahi, Sidra DeKoven. 1996. "Representing Auschwitz." *History and Memory* 7, no. 2 (Fall): 121–64.

Ferro, Marc. 1987. *Pétain.* Paris: Fayard.

Fine, Ellen. 1982. *Legacy of Night: The Literary Universe of Elie Wiesel.* Albany: State Univ. of New York Press.

Finkielkraut, Alain. 1998. "Serge Klarsfeld, le fou de la mémoire." *Le Monde*, 3 Feb.

———. 2002. *L'Imparfait du présent.* Paris: Gallimard.

Fredriksen, Paula. 2000a. "Allegory and Reading God's Book: Paul and Augustine on the Destiny of Israel." In *Interpretation and Allegory: Antiquity to the Modern Period*, edited by Jon Whitman, 123–47. Leiden: Brill.

———. 2000b. "Patristic *Pramā* and *Pramāṇa*: Augustine and the Quest for Truth." In *Religious Truth: A Volume in the Comparison of Religious Ideas*, edited by Robert C. Neville et al., 109–26. Albany: State Univ. of New York Press.

Friedman, Richard Elliot. 1995. "The Hiding of the Face: An Essay on the Literary Unity of the Biblical Narrative." In *Judaic Perspectives on Ancient Israel*, edited by J. Neusner, B. A. Levine, and E. S. Frerichs, 207–22. Philadelphia: Fortress Press.

Ganzfried, Daniel. 1998a. "Die Geliehene Holocaust-Biographie." *Weltwoche*, 27 Aug.

———. 1998b. "Fakten gegen Erinnerung." *Weltwoche*, 3 Sept.

———. 1998c. "Bruchstücke und Scherbenhaufen." *Weltwoche*, 24 Sept.

Gary, Romain. 1979. *La Bonne moitié.* Paris: Gallimard.

Gates, Henry Louis Jr. 1991. " 'Authenticity,' or the Lesson of Little Tree." *New York Times Book Review*, 14 Nov.

Geller, Jay. "Preface." *American Imago* 59, no. 3 (Fall 2002).

Gilbert, Martin. 1985. *The Holocaust: A History of the Jews of Europe During the Second World War.* New York: Henry Holt.

Gourevitch, Philip. 1999. "The Memory Thief." *New Yorker,* 14 June, 48–68.

Gopnik, Adam. 1998. "Papon's Paper Trail." *New Yorker,* 27 Apr. and 4 May, 90.

Green, Arthur. 1996. "Three Warsaw Mystics." In *Jerusalem Studies in Jewish Thought.* Vol. 13, *Rivkah Shatz-Uffenheimer Memorial Volume,* edited by R. Elior and J. Dan, 1–58. Jerusalem: Hebrew Univ.

Greilsamer, Laurence. 1997. "Maurice Papon, une carrière française." *Le Monde,* 1 Oct.

Haber, Ludwig Frizt. 1986. *The Poisonous Cloud: Chemical Warfare in the First World War.* Oxford: Oxford Univ. Press.

Hanks, Robert. 1996. Review of Wilkomirski, *Fragments. The Independent* (London), 8 Dec.

Harrison, Tony. 1992. *Square Rounds.* London: Faber and Faber.

Harrowitz, Nancy. 1998. "From Mt. Sinai to the Holocaust: Primo Levi and the Crisis of Science in *The Periodic Table.*" In *Celebrating Elie Wiesel: Stories, Essays, Reflections,* edited by Alan Rosen, 19–39. Notre Dame, Ind.: Univ. of Notre Dame Press.

Henry-Haye, Gaston. 1972. *La Grande éclipse franco-américaine.* Paris: Plon.

Heschel, Susannah. 1997. Review of Wilkomirski, *Fragments. Tikkun,* 13 Mar.

Hirsch, Marianne. 1997. *Family Frames: Photography, Narrative, and Postmodernity.* Cambridge, Mass.: Harvard Univ. Press.

Hobbes, Thomas. [1651] 1982. *Leviathan.* New York: Penguin Classics.

ibn Gabbai, R. Meir. 1992. *Avodat ha-Kodesh.* Jerusalem: Shvilei Orchot HaChaim.

Isacovici, Salomon, and Juan Manuel Rodriguez. 1990. *Man of Ashes.* Champaign: Univ. of Illinois Press.

Kedushat Levi on Exod. 2:25 Parashat Shemot, s.v. *"o yevo'ar va-yar'";* p. 87 in the Jerusalem 1978 ed.

Kozol, Jonathan. 1996. Review of Wilkomirski, *Fragments. The Nation,* 28 Oct.

Lanzmann, Claude. 1998. "Y a-t-il une réparation possible, une sanction adéquate pour cette perte immense?" Interview in *Le Monde,* 1 Apr.

Lappin, Elena. 1999. "The Man with Two Heads." *Granta* 66:9–65.

Laub, Dori. 1992. "Bearing Witness or the Vicissitudes of Listening." In *Testimony: Crises of Witnessing in Literature, Psychoanalysis, and History*, edited by Shoshana Felman and Dori Laub. New York: Routledge.

Lejeune, Philippe. 1975. *Le pacte autobiographique*. Paris: Seuil.

Levinas, Emmanuel. 1996. *Proper Names*. Translated by Michael Smith. Stanford, Calif.: Stanford Univ. Press.

Levi, Primo. 1965. *The Reawakening: A Liberated Prisoner's Long March Through Eastern Europe*. Translated by Stuart Woolf. Boston: Little, Brown.

———. 1981. *La ricerca delle radici*. Torino: Einaudi.

———. 1984. *The Periodic Table*. Translated by Raymond Rosenthal. New York: Schocken.

———. 1988. *The Drowned and the Saved*. Translated by Raymond Rosenthal. New York: Summit Books.

———. 1989. "Hatching the Cobra." *The Mirror Maker: Stories and Essays*. Translated by Raymond Rosenthal. New York: Schocken.

———. 1990. *The Sixth Day and Other Tales*. Translated by Raymond Rosenthal. New York: Summit Books.

———. 1996. *Survival in Auschwitz*. Translated by Stuart Woolf. New York: Simon and Schuster.

———. 2001. *A Search for Roots*. Translated by Peter Forbes. London: Penguin.

Lifton, Robert J., and Eric Markusen. 1992. *The Genocidal Mentality: Nazi Holocaust and Nuclear Threat*. New York: Basic Books.

Maechler, Stefan. 2001. *The Wilkomirski Affair: A Study in Biographical Truth*. Translated by John E. Woods. New York: Schocken.

Markus, R. A. 1970. "Augustine: Reason and Illumination." In *Cambridge History of Later Greek and Early Medieval Philosophy*, edited by A. H. Armstrong, 362–73. Cambridge: Cambridge Univ. Press.

Mehlman, Jeffrey. 1995. "The Holocaust Comedies of 'Emile Ajar.'" In *Genealogies of the Text: Literature, Politics, and Psychoanalysis in Modern France*. Cambridge: Cambridge Univ. Press.

McCourt, Frank. 1996. *Angela's Ashes*. New York: Scribner.

Midrash Psalms, on Psalm 123:1. 1995. *Mei ha-Shilo'ah, Likkutei ha-Shas, Berakhot 11b*, s.v. *Hitkinu.* Jerusalem: Bnei Brak.

Miles, Jack. 1995. *God: A Biography.* New York: Vintage.

Muffs, Yochanan. 1992. "Who Will Stand in the Breach? A Study of Prophetic Intercession." *Love and Joy: Law, Language and Religion in Ancient Israel.* New York: Jewish Theological Seminary.

New York Times. 1999. "Publisher Drops Holocaust Book," 3 Nov., B2.

Nora, Pierre. 1997. "Tout concourt aujourd'hui au souvenir obsédant de Vichy." *Le Monde,* 1 Oct.

O'Donnell, James J. 1992. *Augustine: Confessions.* 3 vols. Oxford: Clarendon Press.

Péan, Pierre. 1994. *Une jeunesse française: François Mitterand, 1934–1947.* Paris: Fayard.

Perec, Georges. 1975. *W ou le souvenir d'enfance.* Paris: Denoel.

Proctor, Robert N. 1992. "Racial Medicine and Human Experimentation." In *The Nazi Doctors and the Nuremberg Code: Human Rights in Human Experimentation.* New York: Oxford Univ. Press.

Quindlen, Anna. 1997. "How Dark? How Stormy? I Can't Recall." *New York Times Book Review,* 11 May.

Rawidowicz, Simon. 1974. "Israel's Two Beginnings." In *Studies in Jewish Thought,* ed. Nahum N. Glatzer, 81–209. Philadelphia: Jewish Publication Society.

Ricks, Christopher. 1990. "Literature and the Matter of Fact." University lecture, Boston University, delivered Oct. 30; also included in his *Essays in Appreciation* (Oxford: Oxford University Press: 1996).

———. 1996. *Essays in Appreciation.* Oxford: Oxford Univ. Press.

Ricoeur, Paul. 1983–85. *Temps et récit.* 3 vols. Paris: Editions du Seuil.

Robbe-Grillet, Alain. 1984. *Le miroir qui revient.* Paris: Eds. de Minuit.

———. 1987. *Angélique ou l'enchantement.* Paris: Eds. de Minuit.

———. 1994. *Les derniers jours de Corinthe.* Paris: Eds. de Minuit.

Rousso, Henry. 1991. *The Vichy Syndrome: History and Memory in France since 1944.* Translated by Arthur Goldhammer. Cambridge: Harvard Univ. Press.

———. 1998. "Le tribunal de l'Histoire a jugé Vichy depuis longtemps." Interview in *Le Monde*, 7 Apr.

Schlink, Bernhard. 1997. *The Reader*. New York: Vintage.

Sebald, W. G. 1996. *The Emigrants*. Translated by Michael Hulse. New York: New Directions.

Shatz, Moshe, ed. 1997. *Bei'ur Eser Sefirot*. Jerusalem: n.p.

Slotki, I. W., ed. 1961. *Soncino Talmud*. London: Soncino.

Squire, L. R., et al. 1990. "Memory: Organization of Brain Systems and Cognition." In *Symposium on Quantitative Biology: The Brain*. Vol. 55. Woodbury, N.Y.: Cold Spring Harbor Press.

Steiner, George. 1981. *The Portage to San Cristóbal of A. H.* New York: Simon and Schuster.

Stern, Fritz. 1999. *Einstein's German World*. Princeton, N.J.: Princeton Univ. Press.

Sternberg, Meir. 1985. *The Poetics of Biblical Narrative*. Bloomington: Indiana Univ. Press.

Styron, William. 1979. *Sophie's Choice*. New York: Random House.

Suleiman, Susan Rubin. 2001. "Charlatan or Madman? What a Study of a Literary Hoax Can't Decide." Review of Stefan Maechler, *The Wilkomirski Affair*, *The Forward*, 8, 10, 14 June.

———. 2006. *Crises of Memory and the Second World War*. Cambridge, Mass.: Harvard Univ. Press.

Talmon, Shemaryahu. 1987. "Ezra and Nehemia." In *The Literary Guide to the Bible*, edited by Robert Alter and Frank Kermode. Cambridge, Mass.: Harvard Univ. Press.

Thion, Serge. 1998. "Des faussaires et des dupes." Available at http://www.vho.org/aaargh/fran/revu/TI98/TI981011.html.

Todorov, Tzvetan. 1991. "Fictions et vérités." In *Les morales de l'histoire*, 129–60. Paris: Grasset and Fasquelle.

Tulving, E. 1985. "How Many Memory Systems Are There?" *American Psychologist* 40:385–98.

Van Alphen, Ernst. 1997. *Caught by History: Holocaust Effects in Contemporary Art, Literature, and Theory*. Stanford, Calif.: Stanford Univ. Press.

Vidal-Naquet, Pierre. 1998. "Papon acquitté, ce serait Vichy réhabilité." *Le Monde*, 2 Apr.

Wardi, Charlotte. 1996. "Memoire et oubli dans Le Cinquieme Fils et L'Oublie d'Elie Wiesel." In *Une parole pour l'avenir, autour de Elie Wiesel*. Colloque de Cerisy. Paris: Odile Jacob.

Wiesel, Elie. 1958. *La nuit*. Paris: Seuil.

———. 1960. *Night*. New York: Hill and Wang.

———. 1970. *One Generation After*. New York: Random House.

———. 1973. *The Oath*. Translated by Marion Wiesel. New York: Random House.

———. 1976. "The Sacrifice of Isaac: A Survivor's Story." *Messengers of God: Biblical Portraits and Legends*. New York: Summit Books.

———. 1978. *Four Hasidic Masters and Their Struggle Against Melancholy*. Notre Dame, Ind.: Univ. of Notre Dame Press.

———. 1979a. *The Trial of God*. Translated by Marion Wiesel. New York: Random House.

———. 1979b. *A Jew Today*. Translated by Marion Wiesel. New York: Vintage Books.

———. 1981. *The Testament*. Translated by Marion Wiesel. New York: Summit Books.

———. 1982a. *Dawn*. New York: Bantam.

———. 1982b. *Night*. Translated by Stella Rodway. New York: Bantam.

———. 1982c. *Paroles d'étranger: Textes, contes et dialogues*. Paris: Editions du Seuil.

———. 1985a. *A Beggar in Jerusalem*. New York: Schocken.

———. 1985b. *The Fifth Son*. Translated by Marion Wiesel. New York: Summit Books.

———. 1986. *The Nobel Peace Prize 1986*. New York: Summit Books.

———. 1987. *Twilight*. New York: Summit Books.

———. 1992. *The Forgotten*. Translated by Stephen Becker. New York: Summit Books.

———. 1994. *Tous les fleuves vont à la mer: Mémoires I*. Paris: Seuil, collection "Points."

———. 1995a. *All Rivers Run to the Sea: Memoirs*. New York: Alfred A. Knopf.

———. 1995b. *Le passage du témoin*. Brussels: La lettre volée.

———. 1998. *Rencontre avec Elie Wiesel: Le mal et l'exil, Dialogue avec Philippe-Michael de Saint-Cheron*. Paris: Nouvelle Cité.

Wiesel, Elie, and Richard D. Heffner. 2001. *Conversations with Elie Wiesel*. New York: Schocken.

Wilkomirski, Binjamin. 1996. *Fragments: Memories of a Wartime Childhood*. Translated by Carol Brown Janeway. New York: Schocken.

———. 1998. "Niemand muss mir Glauben schenken." *Tages Anzeiger*, 1 Sept.

Yeushson, B. 1956. *Fun Unzer Alten Oytzer*. Vol. 6. New York: Shengold.

Yonnet, Paul. 1993. *Voyage au centre du malaise français: l'antiracisme et le roman national*. Paris: Gallimard.

Young, James E. 1988. *Writing and Rewriting the Holocaust: Narratives and the Consequences of Interpretation*. Bloomington: Indiana Univ. Press.

Index

Aaron (Biblical priest), 111, 139–40
Adam (first man), 135
Against All Hope (Valladares), 61
Agnon, Shamuel Yosef, 116
Aharon Lipkin (fict.), 111
Allen and Unwin (publishers), 8
All Rivers Run to the Sea (Wiesel), 21, 38–42
Alphen, Ernst van, 31
Alzheimer's disease, 55, 117, 127
Amery, Jean, 162
Amidah, 114–15
Angela's Ashes (McCourt), 23–24
"Angelic Butterfly" (Levi), 86
anomaly, 13–14, 15, 18
anti-Semitic Racial Laws (Italy), 100
anti-Semitism: of Demidenko, 7; emergence from scientific community, 89; in France, 74–76; of Holocaust deniers, 62; in Italy, 100; methods used, 159–60; occupation of Poland vs., 17–18; results of, 112, 113
Apollo 13 (film), 60–61
Ariel (fict.), 123–24

Aristotle, 23n. 3, 64
ark of the covenant, 144, 144–45n. 7
artifice, 23–24, 26n. 7
artistry, 23–24, 26n. 7, 27–28, 35–38
assassination of Kennedy, 59
atomic bomb, 88, 89, 94
Augustine of Hippo, xviii, 131–38
Auschwitz: account of train ride to, 39–42; chemistry test, 96–97; explanations of, 160; French Jews sent to, 71; as graveyard of Jewish civilization, 17; Levi's identity crisis in, 84, 100–101; need to remind God of, 117, 119; Polish Christian victims, 12–13; suicide after, 162; survivors of, 100–101; victims of, 12; voice of victims of, 107–8; witnesses to uprising, 31–32; Zyklon-B and, 89
Australian Federation of Ukrainian Organizations, 8
autobiography, 24n. 5
Avihu (son of Aaron), 111
Azriel (fict.), 121
Azriel (Rabbi of Gerona), 147

175

Babi Yar (commemorative site), xvi
Barbie, Klaus, 70, 71n. 4
Bates, W. Jackson, 145n. 7
bat kol, 115, 116
Beaufort, Hubert de, 78n. 29
Beckett, Samuel, 113
Beggar in Jerusalem, A (Wiesel), 113, 116
Berger, Alan L., ix, xvii, 117–28
Bergès, Michel, 79n. 30
Bernstein, Michael-André, 32–33
Bialik, Hayyim Nahman, 109
Bible: book of Ezra, 142, 146; book of Habakkuk, 141, 148–49; book of Nehemiah, xviii, 141–44; Golden Rule of, 56; Hannah's plight in, 140; mediation of knowledge of God through, 138; on memory of God, 139–40; Psalm 19, 108
Blake, William, 113
Bontchek (fict.), 123
Borowski, Tadeus, 162
Bousquet, René, 74–75
Bousquet generation, 74–76
Bousquet-Oberg accords, 73–74
breastplate of judgment, 140
Brecht, Bertolt, 113, 160
Breton, André, 21, 42
Breznitz, Judith, 43–44
Breznitz, Shlomo, ix, xv, 43–51, 57
Buber, Martin, 109

Castagnède, Jean-Louis, 79
Castro, Fidel, 61

categorical boundaries of genre, xiv, 7–11, 25–26, 32–35
catharsis, 110
Celan, Paul, 162
Chapel, Gillette, 77n. 22
Chemical War, 90, 91, 93, 103
chemistry/chemists, 84–85, 89, 90–100, 102–3
circumcision, 139
Cohn, Dorritt, 23n. 3
Cold War revisionists, 62
collaboration: atomic bomb development as, 94; Gatterman's book and, 97–98; of Haber, 90–91, 93, 103; impact on Levi, 84–85, 96, 99–102; of Vichy regime, xvi, 73–78
communal memory, xiv–xv, 151–52
Conan, Eric, 78n. 28
Confessions of Augustine: applicability to modern life, xviii; as introspective autobiography, 131–32; on knowledge of God, 133–35; as meditative triptych, 132–33; on time, 135–38; triple structure of, 133
Confessions of Nat Turner (Styron), 12
contemporary relativism, 5–6
conversion, 92
Creation of Adam, The (Michelangelo), 126
Cronkite, Walter, 61–62

Darville, Helen (a.k.a. Demidenko), 7–8

Index / 177

Dawn (Wiesel), 110
Day of Judgment, 140
death camps: ideology of, 17; use of science in, 89, 92, 94. *See also* Auschwitz
de Gaulle, Charles, 71–72, 73, 77, 78
Demidenko, Helen, 7–8
deniers of Holocaust, 30
Dershowitz, Alan, 7–8
Description de l'île de Formose en Asie (Psalmanazar), 36
Di-Nur, Yehiel, 157
Disney Corporation, 60
distancing, 45–48
Doesseker, Bruno, 10, 28–29
Doubrovsky, Serge, 24n. 5
Drancy (French camp), 71
Dreyfus trial, 80
Drowned and the Saved, The (Levi), 12, 84, 88, 95, 100–102
Druon, Maurice, 78
Dutourd, Jean, 78

Education of Little Tree (Gates), 35n. 16
Ein-Sof, 147–48
Eisenschiml, Otto, 58–59
Eisner, Michael, 60
Elhana Rosenbaum (fict.), 117, 124–25, 127–28
Elisha (fict.), 110
Emigrants, The (Sebald), 23
empathy, 44, 46–48
Enabling Act, 92
Ephraim (fict.), 126–27

episodic memory, 44, 45
ethics, 55, 56, 63–64, 128
European Court of Human Rights, 81
European Jewish civilization, 17
explicit memory, 48
Ezra, 142, 146

fabrication: imagination vs., 64; memory and, 43; movies as, 59–61; photographs as, 61; of revisionists, 62–63. *See also* hoaxes
facts: fiction's obligation to, 64; historical events accepted as, 6; interpretation of, 64; revisionism and, 62–63; truth vs., 22, 36–37
factual accuracy: of *Fragments*, 29–30; impact on reader's experience, 25n. 6; interpretive framework vs., 30–32; problem of translation and, 39–42
Fall of Man, 135–36
father-son relationships, 124–25
fear of the Lord, 108–9, 110, 115
Feuerbach, Ludwig Andreas, 151
fiction: accepted as truth, 24n. 4; as *bat kol*, 115; categorical boundaries of, 32–33; claims of historical truth in, 16; definition of, 23n. 3; factual accuracy in, 25n. 6, 64; history vs., 5–7, 13–14, 15; imperfect recollection of past in, 23; literary elastic license and, 11–13, 14, 16, 18;

fiction (*continued*)
: *Man of Ashes* controversy, 8–9;
memoirs vs., xiv, 5, 22–25; as
mode of silence, 112; morality
of, 113; preparation for future
through, 112; presented as
history, 16; presented as
memoir/autobiography, xiv, 7–11,
26–36; as voice of the dead, 108;
of Wiesel, 108–14, 115–16,
117–28; Wiesel's view of, 123.
See also imagination; *specific fiction title*

fictional impersonation: damage
done by, 10–11; definition of, 7;
by Demidenko, 7–8; by Isacovici,
8–9; by Wilkomirski, 9–11

"Fictions and Truths" (Todorov), 35–37

Fifth Son, The (Wiesel), 110, 120, 122

films: focus of, 16; Holocaust
coverage, 3–5; *Pocahontas* (Disney
film), 60; Wiesel's view of, 123.
See also movies; newsreels

Final Solution, 12, 16–17, 73–75,
88–89, 159–60. *See also*
Holocaust

Fine, Ellen, 121, 122

Finkielkraut, Alain, 81

foreknowledge, 146–47

forgetting, 148n. 12

Forgotten, The (Wiesel): concept of
memory in, xvii, 109, 119, 120;
father-son relationship in, 118,
124–25; portrayal of Alzheimer's
disease, 55; postmemory of, 124;
as prayer, 127–28; theme of
works of, 117

For Those I Loved (Gray), 35

Four Hasidic Masters (Wiesel), 114

Fragments: Memories of a Wartime Childhood
(Wilkomirski): artistry of, 35–38;
awards of, 10, 11, 26; blurring of
boundaries of genre, xiv, 26,
32–35; damage done by, 10–11,
30; existence of Holocaust and,
30, 32–33; perspective of, 27;
questions raised by, 21, 37–38;
reviews of, 26n. 7; story told by,
27–28; verifiability of, 9–11,
28–29n. 8

France: collaboration and resistance
in, xvi, 71, 73–78; influences on
courts of, 71; literary coding in,
79; memory of Holocaust, xvi,
73–76; Papon trial in, 69–71,
72–73, 76–77, 79–81; project of
revolutionary left in, 75–76; war
crime categories, 70–71

fraud. *See* hoaxes

Fredriksen, Paula, ix, xvii, 131–38

freedom of will, 146–47

future, 112

Ganzfried, Daniel, 10, 28–29n. 8, 34

Gary, Romain, 78

Gates, Henry Louis, Jr., 35n. 16

Gattermann, Ludwig, 94–98

Genesis, 151

genocide: documentation of in *Sophie's Choice*, 12; French role in, 73–75; ineffable horrors of, 159–60; magnitude of, 16–17; as result of hate-speech, 113; role of science in, 88–89. *See also* Holocaust
genre: blurring of boundaries of, xiv, 7–11, 21, 23–24, 25–26, 32–34; textual criterion for, 23–24; of Wiesel's works, 113
God: approach to, 115; Augustine's search for knowledge of, 132–33; bitterness toward, 108–9; communal aspects of memory of, 151–52; efforts to justify, 111; fear of, 108–9, 110, 115; of Hasidism, 148–51; hiding of the face of, 142–46; ineffable name of, 120, 159; of Kabbalah, 147–48; memory of, xvii, 109, 139–40, 149–51, 153; memory of Shoah and, 117, 118, 119, 127–28; need for redemption, 109; parable of in *The Forgotten*, 117, 118; reminders from people of, 140–46; response to memories of men, 153; scripture and, 138; as social construct, 150–51; time and, 136–37, 138; voice of, 115; Wiesel's portrayal of, 127
Gray, Martin, 35
Greilsamer, Laurence, 77n. 23
Grisha (fict.), 121, 122
Grosjean, Yvonne Berthe, 10, 29

Habakkuk, 141, 148–49
Haber, Charlotta, 93
Haber, Clara, 92–93
Haber, Fritz, 85, 90–92, 93, 99, 102–3
Haber, Ludwig, 93
Hand That Signed the Papers, The (Demidenko), 7–8
Hanks, Robert, 26n. 7
Hannah (Biblical supplicant), 140
Harrison, Tony, 93
Harrowitz, Nancy, ix, xvi, 83–103
Hartman, Geoffrey, x, xvii, 107–116
Hasidism, 148–51, 152–53
"Hatching the Cobra" (Levi), 84, 86, 94
hate-speech, 113
Hershel (fict.), 126
Heschel, Susannah, 26n. 7
Hilberg, Raoul, 28–29n. 8
Hirsch, Marianne, 118
historical truth, 21, 31
historiography, 5–6
history: anomaly's effect on, 17–18; distortions of, 58–61; fiction vs., 5–7, 13–14, 15; fiction with claims to, 16; gradual transformation of, 58; memory and, xv–xvi, 30–31, 55, 56–58, 63; moral obligation of writers of, 63–64; multiply sources of, 30; revisionists and, 61–63
Hitler, Adolf, 16, 89, 159

hoaxes: definition of, 7, 25–26; *Description de l'île de Formose en Asie*, 36; *The Education of Little Tree* as, 35n. 16; effects of, 37–38; fate of, 35–36; *Fragments: Memories of a Wartime Childhood* as, xiv, 9–11, 26–35; *The Hand That Signed the Papers* as, 7–8; *Man of Ashes* as, 8–9

Hobbes, Thomas, 55

Holocaust: accountability for, 113; big and little stories of, 44–45; children survivors of, 10, 27; command to tell, 123; communication of horrors of, 157–58; defining corollaries of, 17; deniers of, 30, 62; event vs. interpretive framework, 30–32; false revisionists of, 62; fictitious representations of, xiv, 7–13, 26–35, 37–38; Final Solution and, 12, 16–17, 159–60; media and genre representing, xiii; novelistic impersonations and, 7–11; occupation of Poland vs., 17–18; omnipresent memories of, 49–50; ordeal of survivors, 108, 109–10, 120; Polish Christians and, 12–13; role science and technology, 88–89; trivialization of, 37; as ultimate signifier of torments, 37; victims of, 107; voice of victims of, 107–8; Zyklon-B use, 89, 93, 94, 98. *See also* Auschwitz; death camps; Final Solution; genocide

Holocaust deniers, 30, 62

Holocaust museum exits, 50

Holocaust writing: Breton on, 21, 42; hoaxes and frauds, 7–11, 18, 26–31; memory and, 42, 63; nature of, 146; postmodernist view of, 31; suicide and, 161–62; use of literary elastic license, 11–18

Howe, Irving, 37

ideology, 58, 62, 64

illiteracy/literacy, 14–15, 18

imagination: fabrication vs., 64; fraud masquerading as, 7–11; history vs., 5–7, 13–14, 15, 64; literary elastic license as, 12–18; memory and, 55–56

impersonation. *See* fictional impersonation

implicit memory, 48–50

intention of authors, 15–18

Internet, 62–63

interpretive framework, 30–32

Irving, David, 62

Isacovici, Salomon, 8–9

Issahar (fict.), 119

jading of observers, 4

Jeremiah, 141

Jerusalem, 111

Jews: acts against, 16–17, 159–60; Babi Yar commemorative site and, xvi; Enabling Act, 92; Final

Solution and, 12, 16–17, 159–60;
in France during/after World War
II, 75; Haber as, 92–93; Hasidic
view of God's memory, 150–51,
152–53; identification with
spiritual heritage, 116; Kabbalist's
view of God's memory, 147–48;
Levi as, 99–100; response to
catastrophe, 153; revelation
of atrocities against, 3–5, 16;
second-generation identity, 120;
September 11 revisionists and,
62–63; spiritual influence of, 108;
Styron's factual accounts of,
12–13; transportation of from
Bordeaux, 71. *See also* second
generation; witnesses
journalism, 58

Kabbalah, 147–48
Kafka, Franz, 158
Kant, Immanuel, 56, 64
Katz, Steven T., x
Kennedy assassination, 59
Kierkegaard, Soren, 55
Klarsfeld, Arno, 79
Klarsfeld, Serge, 70n. 2, 79
Kosinski, Jerzy, 162
Kozol, Jonathan, 26n. 7
Kraus, Karl, 113

Laden, Osama bin, 63
language, 134, 137–38, 157

Lanzmann, Claude, 70n. 2
Lappin, Elena, 34n. 15, 35
latent memories, xvii, 108, 110, 112,
116
Laub, Dori, 31
Laval, Pierre, 74
Leib, Moshe (Rabbi of Sassov),
149–50
Leiner, Mordechai (Rabbi of Izbica),
151–52
Lejeune, Philippe, 24n. 5
Le miroir qui revient (Robbe-Grillet), 33
Levi, Primo: chemistry exam in
Auschwitz, 96–97; connection to
science, 83–84; on damage to
survivors, 95; description of his
experience, 120; desires from
science, 95–96, 99; identity of,
99–100; literary career, 83,
85–86; omissions of, xvi, 88, 90,
93–94, 98–102; portrayal of
Gattermann, 94–98; portrayal of
science, 85–90, 94; suicide of,
162; validity of words of, 5; on
victims of Auschwitz, 12,
100–101
Levinas, Emmanuel, 116
Lifton, Robert J., 89
Lincoln assassination, 58–59
Lipstadt, Deborah, 62
literary license, 5, 6–7, 11–13, 14,
16, 18
literature, 127
"Literature and the Matter of Fact"
(Ricks), 64

madness, 110–11
Maechler, Stefan, 28–29n. 8, 35, 38n. 18
Maimonides, 147
Malkiel Rosenbaum (fict.), 117, 124–28
Man of Ashes (Isacovici), 8–9
Markusen, Eric, 89
Mauriac, François, 79
McCourt, Frank, 23–24
medieval Jewish philosophers, 146–47
Mehlman, Jeffrey, x, xvi, 69–82
memoirs: advantages of delay in writing, xv, 42, 43–46, 51; categorical boundaries of, 32–33; cost of telling, 50–51; disadvantages of delay in writing, 48–51; factuality and, 21–22, 28–32; fiction vs., xiv, 5, 22–25; history and, 30, 57–58; impact of hoaxes, 38–39; *Man of Ashes* controversy, 8–9; reliability of, xiv, xv, 7–11, 32–33; singular perspective of, 31; tendency toward fiction, 22–24; textual traits of, 23–24; truth claims of, 25–26, 30–31. *See also specific title or author*
memory: alteration of with telling, 50–51; anomaly's effect on, 17–18; Augustine on, 131–38; as bond and barrier, 126–27; centrality of, xviii; claim on God and humanity, 127; communal dimension of God's, 151–52; dilemma of, 118–20; divine-human mirror of, 149; effect of history on, 58–59; effects of revisionists of, 75–76; effects of time on, 57; falsification of, xv–xvi, 7–11, 26–33; fate of at death of witnesses, 117; fiasco of militancy of, 69–82; fiction vs., 5; as fitting response to evil, xvii, 113; foreknowledge and, 146–47; French phases of concerning the war, 73–75; of God, 109, 149–51; God and, xvii–xviii, 139–40; historical truth and, 21, 40, 42; history and, xv–xvi, 30–31, 56–58, 63; imagination and, 55–56; impact of political trials on, xvi, 76; implicit vs. explicit, 48–50; importance of, 55; interpretation of images and, 56; invocation of God's, 140–46; life-giving power of, xvi–xvii, 42, 112; means of contact with time, 55, 137–38; nature of, 147; observation and, 118; omissions of, xvi, 88, 90, 93–94, 98–103; origin of, 135; paradox of, 119–20; purification through, 110; reliability of, xv, 5, 22–23, 102; repression and, 39–40; requirements of, 119; resurrection of the dead through, 108, 110, 112, 116; role of, xvii–xviii, 133; *sefirah Yesod* and, 148n. 12;

semantic vs. episodic, 44; shunning of, 99; significance of, 124, 137, 153; silence and, 121–22; as site of illumination/bridge to God, 133–35; transfusion of, xvii, 111, 116, 117–18, 125–27; tricks played by, 48–51; unconscious manipulation of, 43, 57–58; Wiesel's definition of, 118–19; as Wiesel's theme, 117, 131

Memory Fields (Breznitz): advantages of delay in writing of, 43–48, 51; disadvantages of delay in writing of, 48–51; focus of, 46; temporal distancing of, 45–47

Menahem-Mendel (Rebbe of Kotzk), 158

Michelangelo, 126

militant chemistry, 98–99

Mishneh Torah, 146–47

Mitterrand, François, 72, 75

moon landing, 60

morality of fiction, xvii, 108, 113

Moses, 141, 142

movies, 59–61. *See also* films; newsreels

Muller (chemist at Auschwitz), 85

Mundus novus (Vespucci), 36–37

Nadav (fict.), 111

Nathan Landau (fict.), 12

national identity, xvi, 73–76

Nazis, 16, 73–75, 88–89, 92, 98, 159

negationists, 30

Nehemia (prophet): canonization of his memoir, 152; Hasidic answer to, 150; Kabbalist's answer to, 149; nature of project of, 151; plea for divine recognition, 141–46, 152–53

Nehemia (Biblical Book), xviii, 141–44

nerve gas, 90, 93, 94, 98

newspapers, 3

newsreels, 3

Night (Wiesel), 38–42, 124

nitrogen fixation principles, 90, 91

Noah, 139

Nora, Pierre, 74, 76

novelistic impersonations: *Fragments: Memoirs of a Wartime Childhood* as, 9–11; *The Hand That Signed the Papers* as, 7–8; *Man of Ashes* as, 8–9

novelists: fictional impersonation by, 7–11; literary license of, 6–7, 11–13, 14, 16, 18. *See also specific author*

novels. *See* fiction

Nuremberg Laws, 16

Oath, The (Wiesel), 116, 120, 123

"Of frauds and of dupes" (Thion), 30

One Generation After (Wiesel), 112, 114

Orwell, George, 62, 63

Ozick, Cynthia, x, xiii, 3–18, 55, 56

Paltiel (fict.), 121–22
Pannwitz (chemist in Auschwitz), 97
Papon, Maurice: attempted escape of, 81; contacts with Gaullist resistance, 71; final speech of, 80; health of, 70; imprisonment of, 81–82; as police prefect, 71–72; suit against Einaudi, 72n. 6; suit against France, 81; trial of, xvi, 69–71, 72–73, 76–77, 79–81
Papon v. France, 81
parable of the bull, 86–87, 88–89
Paris Cour d'Appel, 82
Passover Haggadah, 123
Pedro (fict.), 107, 113
Perec, Georges, 33–34
Perillus (fict.), 86–87, 88–89
Periodic Table, The (Levi), 84, 85, 98–99
Pétain, Henri Phillippe, 70, 71, 72, 78
Phalarus (fict.), 86–87, 88–89
photographs: authority of, 5, 18, 56, 61; focus of, 16; impact of, 3–5; memory/imagination as interpreter of, 56; as replacement for reality, 50; use of in fiction, 23; validity of, 5; words vs., xiii, 3–5, 16, 18
Pickett's Charge (Gettysburg), 56–57
pilgrimage ritual, 123, 125–26
Pinhas of Koretz, 114–15
Plath, Sylvia, 37
Plato, 23n. 3, 134
Pliny, 86, 88
Pocahontas (Disney film), 60
Poisonous Cloud, The (L. Haber), 93
Polen, Nehemia, x, xvii, 139–53
Polish Christians, 12–13, 18
Polish occupation, 16–18
political trials, xvi, 69–71, 72–73, 76–77, 79–81
Pontecorvo, Bruno, 88
positivists, 31
postmemory, 118, 120–24, 125, 127–28
postmodernism, 31
posttraumatic stress disorder, 49–50
Practical Handbook for Organic Chemists, A (Gattermann), 94–95, 97–98
practical reason, 64
prayer, 127, 149
precariousness, 115–16
present, 136, 137–38
priests, 144
Proctor, Robert, 89
prophets, 140–41
protest at Renault factory, 75–76
Psalmanazar (pseudo.), 36
purification, 110

Quatuor navigatones (Vespucci), 36–37
Quindlen, Anna, 22–23

rabbinic prayer book, 146
rainbow, 139

Raphael (fict.), 110–11
Rawicz, Piotr, 162
Reader, The (Schlink), 11–12, 14, 16, 18
Reawakening, The (Levi), 83
referentiality, 25–26
reflection, 46–48
relativism, 5–6
repression, 39–40
resistance, xvi, 71, 75, 76–78
resurrection of the dead, 107, 108, 110, 112, 116
Reuven (fict.), 122, 123
revisionists, 61–63
Ricks, Christopher, 25n. 6, 64
Robbe-Grillet, Alain, 33
Rodriguez, Juan Manuel, 8–9
Rosen, Alan, x–xi
Rosh Hashanah, 140, 149–50
Ryle, Martin, 88

Sam (fict.), 113
Samarkand story, 47–48
Samuelson, Arthur, 34n. 15
satire, 4
Schlink, Bernhard, 11–12, 14, 16, 18
Schocken Books, 10, 28n. 8, 34n. 15
science: as escape from situations, 96; Gattermann's book, 94–95, 97–98; Haber's contributions to, 90–92, 99, 102–3; Levi's connection to, 83–84; Levi's expectations of, 95–96, 99; Levi's portrayal of, xvi, 85–90, 94; role in World War I, 90, 91, 93, 103; role in World War II, 86, 88–89
scripture, 138
"Scrolls, Too, Are Mortal, The" (Wiesel), 119
Search for Roots, A (Levi), 94–96, 98
Sebald, W. G., 23
second generation: identity of, 120; influence of dead on, 110; of persecutors represented in *The Reader*, 14–15; pilgrimages of, 123, 125–26; postmemory and, 120–24; task of, 118, 124, 125, 128; transfusion of memory to, 117–18, 125–27
second temple, 144–46
Second Temple Judaism, 144–45n. 7
sefirot, 147
Seguin, Philippe, 72n. 8
semantic memory, 44–45
September 11, 2001, attacks, 62–63
sexual continence, 135
Shakespeare, William, 113
Shekhinah, 144n. 6
Shema, 127
Shem-Tov, Rebbe Israel Baal, 114
Silber, John, xi, xv–xvi, 55–65
silence, 158–59
Simha the Dark (fict.), 123
sin, 135
Solomon's temple, 144
Sophie (fict.), 12, 13–14, 16, 17–18
Sophie's Choice (Styron), 11–14, 16, 17–18
Spanish Civil War, The (Thomas), 61

Square Rounds (Harrison), 93
Stanton, Edwin M., 58–59
Stavans, Ilan, 9
Steiner, George, 76
Stern, Fritz, 93
Sternberg, Meir, 25
Stingo (fict.), 12
Stone, Oliver, 59, 63
strange fire, 111
Styron, William, 11–14, 16, 17–18
Suhrkamp Verlag (publisher), 9–10, 28n. 8
Suleiman, Susan Rubin, xi, xiv, 21–42
Survival in Auschwitz (Levi), 83, 84, 96
survivor testimony. *See* witnesses
symbolic figures, 16

tabernacle, 144
Talmudic rabbis, 142
Tanakh: book of Ezra, 142, 146; book of Habakkuk, 141, 148–49; book of Nehemiah, xviii, 141–44; Hannah's plight in, 140; on memory of God, 139–40; Psalm 19, 108
temple, 144–46
temporal distancing, 45–48
Testament, The (Wiesel), 120, 121–22
testimonies. *See* witnesses
theodicy, 109, 113
therapy-induced memory recovery, 10–11
Thion, Serge, 30
Thomas, Hugh, 61

time: control of, 63; God's existence outside of, 136–37, 138, 139; God's investment in, 148–49; imagination as necessary for life in, 56; man's existence within, 135–36, 137; means of contact with, 55; memory and, 55, 57, 110; necessity of memory for life in, 137–38; scriptural bridge to, 138
Todorov, Tzvetan, 35–37
Touvier, Paul, 70, 71n. 4
translations, 39–42
trauma studies, 120
Trial of God, The (Wiesel), 113
trials: of Papon, xvi, 69–71, 72–73, 76–77, 79–81; purpose of, 69–70
truth: ethical search for, 64; facts vs., 22, 31, 36–37; God as, 133–35; history as witness to, 63–64; literary license and, 11–13, 14, 16, 18; of scripture, 138
truth claims, 25, 31, 34–35
truth value, 25n. 6
Twilight (Wiesel), 107, 109, 110–11, 113
typicality, 13–14, 15

United States, 73
University of Nebraska Press, 9
Urim and Thummim, 144

Valladares, Armando, 61
"Veramina" (Levi), 86

verifiability: of *The Forward*, 9; of *Fragments*, 9–10, 28–29; of *The Hand That Signed the Papers*, 7–8; requirement of memoirs, 25–26
Vespucci, Amerigo, 36–37
Vichy regime, 70, 73–75, 76–78, 80
Vrba, Rudolf, 30

Wardi, Charlotte, 122, 124–25
Weitzmann, Chaim, 92
Wiesel, Elie: acceptance of Nobel Peace Prize, 107; *All Rivers Run to the Sea*, 21, 38–42; bar mitzvah of, 114; *Beggar in Jerusalem, A*, 113, 116; break with Mitterrand, 75; characters created by, 108, 109–11, 113, 117, 121–27; on comprehension of Holocaust, 44; *Dawn*, 110; on dilemma of telling the tale, 157–62; *Fifth Son, The*, 110, 120, 122; *Forgotten, The*, xvii, 55, 109, 119, 120, 124–28; *Four Hasidic Masters*, 114; on graves of Holocaust victims, 107; greatness of, 63; indivisibility of literature and prayer to, 127; on Isaac, 80; on memory, xi, 118–19, 120; morality of fiction of, xvii; *Night*, 38–42, 124; *Oath, The*, 116, 120, 121, 123; *One Generation After*, 112, 114; pledge of, 108; portrayal of Alzheimer's disease, 55; portrayal of survivors, 108; potency of memory in work of, xvii; purpose of survival of, 116; purpose of works of, 116, 131; reason for not witnessing against Papon, 69n. 1; response to, 115–16; rewriting of Holocaust experience, xiv, 38–42; "Scrolls, Too, Are Mortal, The," 119; task of, 120; *Testament, The*, 120, 121–22; theme of works of, 117, 119–20, 138, 160; *Trial of God, The*, 113; *Twilight*, 107, 109, 110–11, 113; on validity of events, 58, 65; validity of works of, 5, 30; on witnesses, 119
Wiesel, Marion, 42n. 20
Wilkomirski, Binjamin: accusations against, 28–29n. 8, 34–35; blurring of boundaries of genre, xiv, 26, 32–35; true identity of, 10, 28–29; validity of work of, 9–11, 21, 26; value of work of, 37
Wilkomirski Affair, The (Maechler), 38n. 18
Winston Smith (fict.), 62
Wirzberg, Benno, 162
witnesses: despair of, 161–62; effectiveness of Wiesel as, 112; hearer as, 119, 121; impossible task of, 120; inability of, 157, 158–59, 160; mortality of, 56–57, 63, 117; negationist view of, 30; reception of, 5; silence of, 158; usurpation of life of, 8–9

words: corruption of, 18; evocation of memories by, 49; guilt and, 112–13; as hoaxes, 7–11; images vs., viii, 3–5, 16, 18; impotence of, 113–16, 120, 157, 162; interpretation of photographs with, 56; literary license and, 11–13, 14, 16, 18; transformation of, 115; validity of, 5–6. *See also* language; witnesses; writing

World Trade Center, 62–63

World War I, 90–91, 93, 103

World War II: French role in genocide, 73–75; German occupation of France, 73; Polish occupation, 16–18; survival and duplicity during, 76–78; use of science and technology, 86, 87–88, 96, 98; Vichysto-résistant, 78. *See also* Auschwitz; death camps; Holocaust

W or The Childhood Memory (Perec), 33–34

writing: Breton on, 21, 42; distinction between fiction and nonfiction, 24–25; hoaxes and frauds, 7–11, 18, 26–31; memory and, 42, 63; nature of, 21, 146; postmodernist view, 31; suicide and, 161–62; use of literary elastic license, 11–13, 14, 16, 18. *See also* fiction; memoirs; words

Wulf, Josef, 162

Yitzhak, Levi (Rabbi of Berditchev), 148–49

Young, James, 37, 42

Zelig (fict.), 111n. 1

Zupanev (fict.), 122

Zyklon-B, 89, 93, 94, 98